SIR GAWAIN &

THE GREEN KNIGHT

A Modernisation by

A. S. KLINE

POETRY IN TRANSLATION
www.poetryintranslation.com

Please direct sales or editorial enquiries to:
tonykline@poetryintranslation.com

This print edition is published by
Poetry In Translation (*www.poetryintranslation.com*),
via On-Demand Publishing LLC, (a Delaware limited liability Company that does
business under the name "CreateSpace") in partnership with
Amazon Services UK Limited (a UK limited company with registration number
03223028 and its registered office at 60 Holborn Viaduct, London, Greater
London, EC1A 2BN, UK)

ISBN-10: 1973985977
ISBN-13: 978-1973985976

ABOUT THIS WORK

ritten in Middle English of the late Fourteenth Century, Sir Gawain and the Green Knight survives in a single manuscript which also contains three religious poems including Pearl, written it seems by the same author, who is therefore referred to as The Pearl Poet.

The poem tells the story of an incident at the court of King Arthur, involving Sir Gawain's acceptance of a challenge from the mysterious Green Knight, and leading to a test of his chivalry and courage. The poem is a lively, atmospheric, and cleverly-paced example of a quest tale, from which the hero emerges chastened and wiser, and contains an interesting mix of Celtic, French and English motifs. There are many and varied interpretations of the themes and symbols contained in the story, and echoes are found in many other folklore tales and legends.

The Pearl Poet appears to have been a Fourteenth Century contemporary of Chaucer, and the dialect in which the poem is written suggests an origin in the English West Midlands. The poem is written in an alliterative style, in variable length stanzas, their lines containing two pairs of stressed syllables, and each stanza ending in a rhyming quatrain. It is seen as an example of work produced during the Alliterative Revival of the period, but by combining alliteration and rhyme leads forward to the flexible rhymed and unrhymed verse of later times. Various attempts have been made to identify the Pearl Poet with a historical personage but no candidate has been generally accepted.

CONTENTS

The Book of Romance (p132, 1902)
Andrew Land (1844-1912)
Internet Archive Book Images

PART I

I

Soon as the siege and assault had ceased at Troy,
the burg broken and burnt to brands and ashes,
the traitor who trammels of treason there wrought
was tried for his treachery, the foulest on earth.
It was Aeneas the noble and his high kin
who then subdued provinces, lords they became,
well-nigh of all the wealth in the Western Isles:
forth rich Romulus to Rome rapidly came,
with great business that burg he builds up first,
and names it with his name, as now it has;
Ticius to Tuscany, and townships begins;
Langobard in Lombardy lifts up homes;
and fared over the French flood Felix Brutus
on many banks all broad Britain he settles
                then,
        where war and wreck and wonder
        betimes have worked within,
        and oft both bliss and blunder
        have held sway swiftly since.

2

 nd when this Britain was built by this baron rich,

bold men were bred therein, of battle beloved,

in many a troubled time turmoil that wrought.

More flames on this fold have fallen here oft

than any other I know of, since that same time.

But of all that here built, of Britain the kings,

ever was Arthur highest, as I have heard tell.

And so of earnest adventure I aim to show,

that astonishes sight as some men do hold it,

an outstanding action of Arthur's wonders.

If you will list to this lay but a little while,

I'll tell it straight, as I in town heard it,

       with tongue;

    as it was said and spoken

    in story staunch and strong,

    with linked letters loaded,

    as in this land so long.

3

his king lay at Camelot nigh on Christmas
with many lovely lords, of leaders the best,
reckoning of the Round Table all the rich brethren,
with right ripe revel and reckless mirth.
There tourneyed tykes by times full many,
jousted full jollily these gentle knights,
then carried to court, their carols to make.
For there the feast was alike full fifteen days,
with all the meat and mirth men could devise:
such clamour and glee glorious to hear,
dear din in the daylight, dancing of nights;
all was happiness high in halls and chambers
with lords and ladies, as liked them all best.
With all that's well in the world were they together,
the knights best known under the Christ Himself,
and the loveliest ladies that ever life honoured,
and he the comeliest king that the court rules.
For all were fair folk and in their first age
           still,
       the happiest under heaven,
       king noblest in his will;
       that it were hard to reckon
       so hardy a host on hill.

'*Jousted full jollily these gentle knights*'
The Boy's King Arthur (p246, 1922)
Sidney Lanier (1842-1881), Newell Convers Wyeth (1882-1945)
Wikimedia Commons

4

hile New Year was so young it was new come in,
that day double on the dais was the dole served,
for the king was come with knights into the hall,
and chanting in the chapel had chimed to an end.
Loud cry was there cast of clerics and others,
Noel nurtured anew, and named full oft;
and see the rich run forth to render presents,
yelled their gifts on high, yield them to hand,
argued busily about those same gifts.
Ladies laughed out loud, though they had lost,
while he that won was not wrath, that you'll know.
All this mirth they made at the meal time.
When they had washed well they went to be seated,
the best of the barons above, as it seemed best;
with Guinevere, full gaily, gracing their midst,
dressed on the dais there, adorned all about –
splendid silk by her sides, and sheer above
of true Toulouse, of Tartar tapestries plenty,
that were embroidered, bright with the best gems
that might be price-proved with pennies
　　　　　any a day.
　　　the comeliest to descry
　　　glanced there with eyen grey;
　　　a seemlier ever to the sight,
　　　sooth might no man say.

'*Guinevere, full gaily, gracing their midst*'
Idylls of the King (p36, 1913)
Baron Alfred Tennyson (1809-1892), Eleanor Fortescue-
Brickdale (1872-1945)
The Internet Archive

5

ut Arthur would not eat till all were served,
he was so joyous a youth, and somewhat boyish:
he liked his life lively, he loved the less
either to long lie idle or to long sit,
so busied him his young blood and his brain wild.
And also another matter moved him so,
that he had nobly named he would never eat
on such dear days, before he had been advised,
of some adventurous thing, an unknown tale,
of some mighty marvel, that he might believe,
of ancestors, arms, or other adventures;
or else till someone beseeched for some sure knight
to join with him in jousting, in jeopardy to lay,
lay down life for life, allow each to the other,
as fortune might favour them, a fair advantage.
This was the king's custom when he in court was,
at each fine feast among his many friends
       in hall.
   Therefore with fearless face
   he stands straight and tall;
   full lively at that New Year
   much mirth he makes with all.

6

hus there stands straight and tall the king himself,

talking at the high table of trifles full courtly.

There good Gawain was graced by Guinevere beside,

and Agravain *a la dure main* on the other side sits,

both the king's sister-sons and full sure knights;

Bishop Baldwin above, he begins the table,

and Ywain, Urien's son, ate alongside him.

These sat high on the dais and deftly served,

and many another sat sure at the side-tables.

Then the first course came with crack of trumpets,

with many a banner full bright that thereby hung;

new noise of kettledrums and noble pipes,

wild warbles and wide wakened echoes,

that many a heart full high heaved at their notes.

Dainties drawn in therewith of full dear meats,

foods of the freshest, and in such files of dishes

they find no room to place them people before

and to set the silver that holds such servings

on cloth.

Each his load as he liked himself,

there ladled and nothing loath;

Every two had dishes twelve,

good beer and bright wine both.

'*Every two had dishes twelve*'
Idylls of the King (p56, 1898)
Baron Alfred Tennyson (1809-1892), George Woolliscroft Rhead
(1854-1920), Louis Rhead (1857-1926)
The British Library

7

 ow will I of their service say you no more,

for each man may well know no want was there

another noise full new neared with speed,

that would give the lord leave to take meat.

For scarce was the noise not a while ceased,

and the first course in the court duly served,

there hales in at the hall door a dreadful man,

the most in the world's mould of measure high,

from the nape to the waist so swart and so thick,

and his loins and his limbs so long and so great

half giant on earth I think now that he was;

but the most of man anyway I mean him to be,

and that the finest in his greatness that might ride,

for of back and breast though his body was strong,

both his belly and waist were worthily small,

and his features all followed his form made

        and clean.

    Wonder at his hue men displayed,

    set in his semblance seen;

    he fared as a giant were made,

    and over all deepest green.

8

nd all garbed in green this giant and his gear:
a straight coat full tight that stuck to his sides,
a magnificent mantle above, masked within
with pelts pared pertly, the garment agleam
with blithe ermine full bright, and his hood both,
that was left from his locks and laid on his shoulders;
neat, well-hauled hose of that same green
that clung to his calves and sharp spurs under
of bright gold, on silk stockings rich-barred,
and no shoes under sole where the same rides.
And all his vesture verily was bright verdure,
both the bars of his belt and other bright stones,
that were richly rayed in his bright array
about himself and his saddle, on silk work,
it were tortuous to tell of these trifles the half,
embroidered above with birds and butterflies,
with gay gaudy of green, the gold ever inmost.
The pendants of his harness, the proud crupper,
his bridle and all the metal enamelled was then;
the stirrups he stood on stained with the same,
and his saddle bows after, and saddle skirts,
ever glimmered and glinted all with green stones.
The horse he rode on was also of that hue,

       certain:

    A green horse great and thick,
    a steed full strong to restrain,
    in broidered bridle quick –
    to the giant he brought gain.

'A steed full strong to restrain'
The poetical works of Sir Walter Scott (p164, 1888)
Sir Walter Scott (1771-1832) and William James Rolfe (1827-
1910), Editor
Internet Archive Book Images

9

ell garbed was this giant geared in green,

and the hair of his head like his horse's mane.

Fair fanned-out flax enfolds his shoulders;

A beard big as a bush over his breast hangs,

that with the haul of hair that from his head reaches

was clipped all round about above his elbows,

that half his hands thereunder were hid in the wise

of a king's broad cape that's clasped at his neck.

The mane of that mighty horse was much alike,

well crisped and combed, with knots full many

plaited in thread of gold about the fair green,

here a thread of the hair, and there of gold.

The tail and his forelock twinned, of a suit,

and bound both with a band of a bright green,

dressed with precious stones, as its length lasted;

then twined with a thong, a tight knot aloft,

where many bells bright of burnished gold ring.

Such a man on a mount, such a giant that rides,

was never before that time in hall in sight of human

      eye.

    He looked as lightning bright,

    said all that him descried;

    it seemed that no man might

    his mighty blows survive.

10

nd yet he had no helm nor hauberk, neither,

nor protection, nor no plate pertinent to arms,

nor no shaft, nor no shield, to strike and smite,

but in his one hand he held a holly branch,

that is greatest in green when groves are bare,

and an axe in his other, one huge, monstrous,

a perilous spar to expound in speech, who might.

The head of an ell-rod its large length had,

the spike all of green steel and of gold hewn,

the blade bright burnished with a broad edge

as well shaped to sheer as are sharp razors.

The shaft of a strong staff the stern man gripped,

that was wound with iron to the wand's end,

and all engraved with green in gracious workings;

a cord lapped it about, that linked at the head,

and so around the handle looped full oft,

with tried tassels thereto attached enough

on buttons of the bright green broidered full rich.

This stranger rides in and the hall enters,

driving to the high dais, danger un-fearing.

Hailed he never a one, but high he overlooked.

The first word that he spoke: 'Where is,' he said,

'the governor of this throng? Gladly I would

see that soul in sight and with himself speak

　　　　reason.'

　　　On knights he cast his eyes,

　　　And rolled them up and down.

　　　He stopped and studied ay

　　　who was of most renown.

II

here was a looking at length the man to behold,

for each man marvelled what it might mean

for a rider and his horse to own such a hue

as grew green as the grass and greener it seemed,

than green enamel on gold glowing the brighter.

All studied that steed, and stalked him near,

with all the wonder of the world at what he might do.

for marvels had they seen but such never before;

and so of phantom and fairie the folk there it deemed.

Therefore to answer was many a knight afraid,

and all stunned at his shout and sat stock-still

in a sudden silence through the rich hall;

as all had slipped into sleep so ceased their noise

    and cry.

    I think it not all in fear,

    but some from courtesy;

    to let him all should revere

    speak to him firstly.

12

hen Arthur before the high dais that adventure beholds,
and, gracious, him reverenced, a-feared was he never,
and said: 'Sir, welcome indeed to this place,
the head of this house, I, Arthur am named.
Alight swiftly adown and rest, I thee pray,
and what thy will is we shall wait after.'
'Nay, so help me,' quoth the man, 'He that on high sits:
to wait any while in this way, it was not my errand.
But as the light of thee, lord, is lifted so high,
and thy burg and thy barons the best, men hold,
strongest under steel gear on steeds to ride,
the wisest and worthiest of the world's kind,
proof to play against in other pure sports,
and here is shown courtesy, as I have heard said,
so then I wandered hither, indeed, at this time.
You may be sure by this branch that I bear here
that I pass by in peace and no plight seek.
For were I found here, fierce, and in fighting wise,
I had a hauberk at home and a helm both,
a shield and a sharp spear, shining bright,
and other weapons to wield, I well will, too;
but as I wish no war, I wear the softer.
But if you be as bold as all bairns tell,
you will grant me goodly the gift that I ask
                by right.'
            Arthur answered there,
            and said: 'Sir courteous knight,
            if you crave battle bare,
            here fails you not the fight.'

13

'Nay, follow I no fight, in faith I thee tell.

About on these benches are but beardless children;

if I were clasped in armour on a high steed,

here is no man to match me, his might so weak.

From thee I crave in this court a Christmas gift,

for it is Yule and New Year, and here many young men.

If any so hardy in this house holds himself,

is so bold of blood, hot-brained in his head,

that dare staunchly strike a stroke for another,

I shall give him as gift this weapon so rich,

this blade, that is heavy enough to handle as he likes,

and I will bear the first blow, as bare as I sit.

If any friend be so fell as to fare as I say,

Leap lightly to me; latch on to this weapon –

I quit claim for ever, he keeps it, his own.

And I will stand his stroke straight, on this floor,

if you will grant me the gift to give him another,

       again;

    and yet give him respite

    a twelvemonth and a day.

    Now hurry, let's see aright

    dare any herein aught say.'

14

f he had stunned them at first, stiller were then
all the host in the hall, the high and the low.
The man on his mount he turned in his saddle,
and roundly his red eyes he rolled about,
bent his bristling brows, burning green,
waving his beard about waiting who would rise.
When none would come to his call he coughed full high,
and cleared his throat full richly, ready to speak:
'What, is this Arthur's house,' quoth the horseman then,
'that all the rumour runs of, through realms so many?
Where now your superiority and your conquests,
your grinding down and your anger, your great words?
Now is the revel and the renown of the Round Table
overthrown with the word of a wanderer's speech,
for all duck down in dread without dint of a blow!'
With this he laughed so loud that the lord grieved;
the blood shot for shame into his fair face
> and there,

> he waxed as wrath as wind;

> so did all that there were.

> The king, so keen by kind,

> then stood that strong man near.

15

nd said: 'Horseman, by heaven you ask as a fool,
and as a folly you fain, to find it me behoves.
I know no guest that's aghast at your great words.
Give me now your weapon, upon God's name,
and I shall bear you the boon you'd be having.'
lightly he leaped to him and caught at his hand;
then fiercely the other fellow on foot alighted.
Now has Arthur his axe, and the helm grips,
and strongly stirs it about, to strike with a thought.
The man before him drew himself to full height,
higher than any in the house by a head and more.
With stern face where he stood he stroked his beard,
and with fixed countenance tugged at his coat,
no more moved or dismayed by mighty blows
than if any man to the bench had brought him a drink
      of wine.
      Gawain, that sat by the queen,
      to the king he did incline:
      'I beseech in plain speech
      that this mêlée be mine'

'*I beseech...that this mêlée be mine*'
The poetical works of Sir Walter Scott (p70, 1888)
Sir Walter Scott (1771-1832) and William James Rolfe (1827-1910), Editor
Internet Archive Book Images

16

'Would you, worthiest lord,' quoth Gawain to the king,

'bid me bow from this bench and stand by you there,

that I without villainy might void this table,

and if my liege lady liked it not ill,

I would come counsel you before your court rich.

For I think it not seemly, as it is true known,

that such an asking is heaved so high in your hall,

that you yourself are tempted, to take it to yourself,

while so many bold men about you on benches sit,

that under heaven, I hope, are none higher of will,

nor better of body on fields where battle is raised.

I am the weakest, I know, and of wit feeblest.

least worth the loss of my life, who'd learn the truth.

Only inasmuch as you are my uncle, am I praised:

No bounty but your blood in my body I know.

And since this thing is folly and naught to you falls,

and I have asked it of you first, grant it to me;

and if my cry be not comely, let this court be free

> of blame.'

>> Nobles whispered around,

>> and after counselled the same,

>> to free the king and crown,

>> and give Gawain the game.

17

hen commanded the king the knight for to rise,
and he readily up-rose and prepared him fair,
knelt down before the king, and caught the weapon;
and he lightly left it him, and lifted up his hand
and gave him God's blessing, and gladly him bade
that his heart and his hand should hardy be, both.
'Take care, cousin,' quoth the king, 'how you set on,
and if you read him aright, readily I trow,
that you shall abide the blow he shall bring after.'
Gawain goes to the giant, with weapon in hand,
and boldly abides him, never bothered the less.
Then to Sir Gawain says the knight in the green:
'Re-affirm we our oaths before we go further.
First I entreat you, man, how are you named,
that tell me truly, then, so trust it I may.'
'In God's faith,' quoth the good knight, 'Gawain am I,
that bear you this buffet, whatever befalls after,
and at this time twelvemonth take from thee another
with what weapon you wilt, and no help from any
          alive.'
    The other replies again:
    'Sir Gawain, may I so thrive,
    if I am not wondrous fain
    for you this blow to drive.'

18

'y God,' quoth the green knight, 'Sir Gawain, I like

That I'll face first from your fist what I found here.

And you have readily rehearsed, with reason full true,

clearly all the covenant that I the king asked,

save that you shall secure me, say, by your troth,

that you shall seek me yourself, where so you think

I may be found upon field, and fetch you such wages

as you deal me today before this dear company.'

'Where should I seek,' quoth Gawain, 'where is your place?

I know nothing of where you walk, by Him that wrought me,

nor do I know you, knight, your court or your name.

But teach me truly the track, tell me how you are named,

and I shall wind all my wit to win me thither;

and that I swear you in truth, and by my sure honour.'

'That is enough this New Year, it needs no more,'

quoth the giant in the green to courteous Gawain:

'if I shall tell you truly, when you have tapped me

and you me smoothly have smitten, I swiftly you teach,

of my house and my home and my own name.

Then may you find how I fare, and hold to your word;

and if I spend no speech, then it speeds you the better,

for you may linger in your land and seek no further –

> but oh!

> > Take now your grim steel to thee,

> > and see how you fell oaks.'

> > 'Gladly, sir, indeed,'

> > quoth Gawain; his axe he strokes.

19

he green knight on his ground graciously stands:
with a little lean of the head, flesh he uncovers;
his long lovely locks he laid over his crown,
and let the naked neck to the stroke show.
Gawain gripped his axe and glanced it on high,
his left foot on the field before him he set,
letting it down lightly light on the naked,
that the sharp of the steel sundered the bones,
and sank through the soft flesh, sliced it in two,
that the blade of the bright steel bit in the ground.
The fair head from the frame fell to the earth,
that folk flailed it with their feet, where it forth rolled;
the blood burst from the body, the bright on the green.
Yet nevertheless neither falters nor falls the fellow,
but stoutly he started forth on strong shanks,
and roughly he reached out, where the ranks stood,
latched onto his lovely head, and lifted it so;
and then strode to his steed, the bridle he catches,
steps into stirrup and strides him aloft,
and his head by the hair in his hand holds.
and as steady and staunch him in his saddle sat
as if no mishap had him ailed, though headless now
> instead.

> He twined his trunk about,
> that ugly body that bled;
> many of him had doubt,
> ere ever his speech was said.

'*The fair head from the frame fell to the earth*'
Enid (p118, 1868)
Baron Alfred Tennyson (1809-1892) and Gustave Doré (1832-1883)
The Internet Archive

20

or the head in his hand he holds up even,

towards the dearest on dais addresses the face;

and it lifted its eyelids, and looked full wide,

and made this much with its mouth, as you may now hear;

'Look, Gawain, be you geared to go as you promised,

and look out loyally till you me, lord, find,

as you swore oath in this hall, these knights hearing.

To the green chapel you go, I charge you, to find

such a dint as you dealt – deserved you have –

to be readily yielded on New Year's morn.

The knight of the green chapel, men know me as, many;

therefore to find me, if you fain it, you'll fail never.

Come then, or be called recreant it behoves you.'

With a rough rasping the reins he twists,

hurled out the hall door, his head in his hand,

that the fire of the flint flew from fleet hooves.

to what land he came no man there knew,

no more than they knew where he had come from

what then?

The king and Gawain there

at that green man laugh and grin;

yet broadcast it was abroad

as a marvel among those men.

'*To what land he came no man there knew*'
The Boy's King Arthur (p82, 1922)
Sidney Lanier (1842-1881), Newell Convers Wyeth (1882-1945)
Wikimedia Commons

21

hough Arthur the high king at heart had wonder,
he let no semblance be seen, but said aloud
to the comely queen, with courteous speech:

'Dear dame, today dismay you never;
well become us these crafts at Christmas,
larking at interludes, to laugh and to sing
among the courtly carols of lords and ladies.
Nevertheless my meat I may now me address,
for I have seen my marvel, I may not deny.'
He glanced at Sir Gawain and graciously said:
'Now sir, hang up your axe that has hewn enough.'
And it adorned the dais, hung on display,
where all men might marvel and on it look,
and by true title thereof to tell the wonder.
Then they went to the board these two together,
the king and the godly knight, and keen men them served
of all dainties double, as dearest might fall,
with all manner of meat and minstrelsy both.
Full well they whiled that day till it worked its end
   on land
  Now think well, Sir Gawain,
  lest by peril unmanned,
  this adventure to sustain,
  you have taken in hand.

PART II

22

 his gift of adventure has Arthur thus on the first
of the young year, for he yearned exploits to hear.
Though words were wanting when they went to sit,
now are they stoked with stern work, fullness to hand.
Gawain was glad to begin those games in hall,
yet if the end be heavy, have you no wonder;
though men be merry in mind when they have strong ale,
a year turns full turn, and yields never a like;
the form of its finish foretold full seldom.
For this Yuletide passed by, and the year after,
and each season slips by pursuing another:
after Christmas comes crabbed Lenten time,
that forces on flesh fish and food more simple.
But then the weather of the world with winter it fights,
cold shrinks down, clouds are uplifted,
shining sheds the rain in showers full warm,
falls upon fair flats, flowers there showing.
Both ground and groves green is their dress,
birds begin to build and brightly sing they
the solace of the soft summer ensuing after
            on bank;
        and blossoms bloom to blow
        by hedges rich and rank,
        while noble notes do flow
        in woodland free and frank.

23

fter, in season of summer with the soft winds,

when Zephyrus sighs himself on seeds and herbs;

well-away is the wort that waxes out there,

when the dunking dew drops from the leaves,

biding a blissful blush of the bright sun.

But then hies Harvest and hardens it soon,

warns it before the winter to wax full ripe;

then drives with drought the dust for to rise,

from the face of the field to fly full high;

wild wind from the welkin wrestles the sun,

the leaves lance then from linden, light on the ground,

and all grey is the grass, that green was ere;

then all ripens and rots, that rose up at first.

And thus wears the year into yesterdays many,

and winter walks again, as the world's way is,

      I gauge,

    till Michaelmas moon

    threatens a wintry age.

    Then thinks Gawain full soon,

    of his wearisome voyage.

24

et till All-Hallows with Arthur he lingers,

and he made a feast on that day for the knight's sake,

with much revel and rich of the Round Table.

Knights full courteous and comely ladies,

all for love of that lad in longing they were;

but nevertheless they named nothing but mirth,

many joyless for that gentle soul jokes made there.

For, after meat, with mourning he makes to his uncle,

and speaks his departure, and openly says:

'Now, liege lord of my life, I ask you leave.

You know the cost in this case, care I no more

to tell you the trial thereof, naught but a trifle;

but I am bound to bear it, be gone, and tomorrow,

to seek the giant in the green, as God will me guide.'

Then the best of the burg were brought together,

Ywain and Eric and others full many,

Sir Dodinal le Sauvage, the Duke of Clarence,

Lancelot and Lionel and Lucan the Good,

Sir Bors and Sir Bedivere, big men both,

and many other men, with Mador de la Porte.

All this courtly company came the king near,

for to counsel the knight, with care in their hearts.

There was much dark dolefulness deep in the hall,

that so worthy as Gawain should wend on that errand,

to endure a dreadful dint, and no more with sword

wander.
The knight made yet good cheer,
and said: 'Why should I falter?
Such destinies foul or fair
what can men do but suffer?'

25

e dwelt there all that day, and dressed on the morn,

asks early for his arms, and all were they brought.

First a crimson carpet, cast over the floor,

and much was the gilded gear that gleamed thereon.

The strong man steps there, and handles the steel,

dressed in a doublet of silk of Turkestan,

and then a well-crafted cape, clasped at the top,

that with a white ermine was trimmed within.

Then set they the plate shoes on his strong feet,

his legs lapped in steel with lovely greaves,

with knee-pieces pinned thereto, polished full clean,

about his knees fastened with knots of gold;

then the cuisses, that cunningly enclosed

his thick-thewed thighs, attached with thongs;

and then the hauberk linked with bright steel rings

over rich wear, wrapped round the warrior;

and well-burnished bracelets over both arms,

elbow-pieces good and gay, and gloves of plate,

and all the goodly gear that should bring him gain

that tide;

with rich coat armour,

his gold spurs set with pride,

girt with a blade full sure

with silk sword-belt at his side.

26

hen he was hasped in armour, his harness was rich;
the least laces or loops gleamed with gold.
So harnessed as he was he hears the Mass,
offered and honoured at the high altar,
then he comes to the king and his companions,
takes his courteous leave of lords and ladies;
and they him kiss and convey, commend him to Christ.
By then Gringolet was game, girt with a saddle
that gleamed full gaily with many gold fringes,
everywhere nailed full new, for that noted day;
the bridle barred about, with bright gold bound;
the apparel of the breast-guard and proud skirts,
crupper, caparison, in accord with the saddle-bows;
and all was arrayed with rich red gold nails,
that all glittered and glinted as gleam of the sun.
Then hefts he the helm, and hastily it kisses,
that was strongly stapled and stuffed within.
It was high on his head, clasped behind,
with a light covering over the face-guard,
embroidered and bound with the best gems
on broad silken border, and birds on the seams,
such as parrots painted preening between,
turtle-doves, true-love knots, so thick entailed
as many burdened with it had been seven winters
            in town.
        The circlet of greater price
        that embellished his crown,
        of diamonds all devised
        that were both bright and brown.

'*So harnessed as he was he hears the Mass*'
The Book of Romance (p101, 1902)
Andrew Land (1844-1912)
Internet Archive Book Images

27

hen they showed him the shield that was of shining gules,
with the pentangle painted there in pure gold hues.
He brandishes it by the baldric, casts it about his neck,
that suited the wearer seemly and fair.
And why the pentangle applies to that prince noble,
I intend to tell, though I tarry more than I should.
It is a sign Solomon settled on some while back,
in token of truth, by the title that it has,
for it is a figure that has five points,
and each line overlaps and locks with another,
and everywhere it is endless, and English call it
over all the land, as I here, the Endless Knot.
For so it accords with this knight and his bright arms,
forever faithful in five ways, and five times so,
Gawain was for good known, and, as purified gold,
void of every villainy, with virtues adorned

        all, so.

      And thus the pentangle new
      he bore on shield and coat,
      as title of trust most true
      and gentlest knight of note.

28

irst he was found faultless in his five senses,
and then failed never the knight in his five fingers,
and all his trust in the field was in the five wounds
that Christ caught on the cross, as the creed tells.
And wheresoever this man in mêlée was stood,
his first thought was that, over all other things,
all his force in fight he found in the five joys
that holy Heaven's Queen had of her child;
for this cause the knight fittingly had
on the inner half of his shield her image painted,
that when he beheld her his boldness never failed.
The fifth five that I find the knight used
was Free-handedness and Friendship above all things;
his Continence and Courtesy corrupted were never,
and Piety, that surpasses all points – these pure five
were firmer founded in his form than another.
Now all these five-folds, forsooth, were fused in this knight,
and each one joined to another that none end had,
and fixed upon five points that failed never,
never confused on one side, nor sundered neither,
without end at any angle anywhere, I find,
wherever its guise begins or glides to an end.
Therefore on his shining shield shaped was the knot
royally with red gold upon red gules,
thus is the pure pentangle called by the people

    of lore.

Now geared was Gawain gay,

lifted his lance right there,

and gave them all good day –

as he thought, for evermore.

29

e struck the steed with the spurs, and sprang on his way

so strongly the stone-fire sparked out thereafter.

All that saw the seemly sight sighed in their hearts,

and said softly the same thing all to each other,

in care of that comely knight: 'By Christ, 'tis pity,

that you, lord, shall be lost, who art of life noble!

To find his fellow in field, in faith, is not easy.

Warily to have wrought would wiser have been,

to have dealt yon dear man a dukedom of worth.

A loyal leader of this land's lances in him well seems,

and so had better have been than brought to naught,

beheaded by an elvish man, out of arrogant pride.

Who knew any king ever such counsel to take

as knights in altercations in Christmas games?'

Well was the water warm much wept from eyen,

when that seemly sire spurred from the court

     that day.

   He made no delay,

   but swiftly went his way;

   Many a wild path he strayed,

   so the books do say.

30

ow rides this knight through the realm of Logres,
Sir Gawain, in God's name, yet no game it thought.
Oft friendless alone he lay long a-nights,
where he found no fare that he liked before him.
He had no friend but his steed by furze and down,
and no one but God to speak with on the way,
till that he neared full nigh to northern Wales.
All the Isle of Anglesey on the left hand he held,
and fared over the fords by the forelands,
over at Holyhead, till he reached the bank
in the wilderness of Wirral – few thereabouts
that either God or other with good heart loved.
And ever he asked as he fared, of fellows he met,
if they had heard any word of a knight in green,
on any ground thereabout, of the green chapel;
and all met him with nay, that never in their lives
saw they ever a sign of such a one, hued

      in green.
    The knight took pathways strange
    by many a bank un-green;
    his cheerfulness would change,
    ere might that chapel be seen.

'*The knight took pathways strange by many a bank un-green*'
The Boy's King Arthur (p214, 1922)
Sidney Lanier (1842-1881), Newell Convers Wyeth (1882-1945)
Wikimedia Commons

31

 any cliffs he over-clambered in countries strange,
far flying from his friends forsaken he rides.
at every twist of the water where the way passed
he found a foe before him, or freakish it were,
and so foul and fell he was beholden to fight.
So many marvels by mountain there the man finds,
it would be tortuous to tell a tenth of the tale.
Sometimes with dragons he wars, and wolves also,
sometimes with wild woodsmen haunting the crags,
with bulls and bears both, and boar other times,
and giants that chased after him on the high fells.
had he not been doughty, enduring, and Duty served,
doubtless he had been dropped and left for dead,
for war worried him not so much but winter was worse,
when the cold clear water from the clouds shed,
and froze ere it fall might to the fallow earth.
Near slain by the sleet he slept in his steel
more nights than enough in the naked rocks,
where clattering from the crest the cold burn runs,
and hung high over his head in hard icicles.
Thus in peril and pain, and plights full hard
covers the country this knight till Christmas Eve
      alone.
    The knight that eventide
    to Mary made his moan,
    to show him where to ride,
    and guide him to some home.

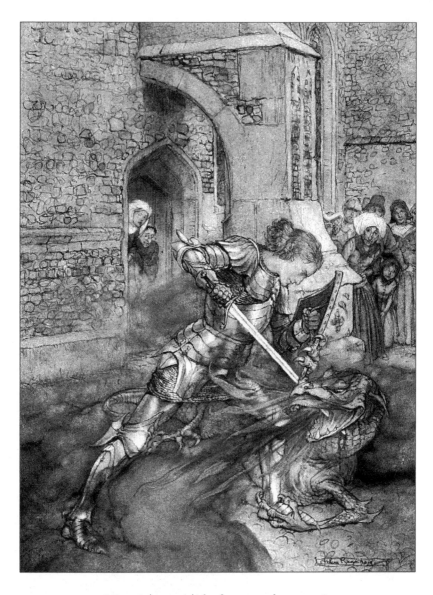

'*Sometimes with dragons he wars*'
The Romance of King Arthur and his Knights of the Round
Table (p360, 1917)
Sir Thomas Malory (15th cent), Alfred William Pollard (1859-
1944), Arthur Rackham (1867-1939)
Internet Archive Book Images

32

y a mount in the morn merrily he rides

into a forest full deep, wonderfully wide,

high hills on either hand, and woodlands under

of hoar oaks full huge a hundred together.

The hazel and the hawthorn were tangled and twined,

with rough ragged moss ravelled everywhere,

with many birds un-blithe upon bare twigs,

that piteously they piped for pinch of the cold.

The gallant on Gringolet glides them under

through many a marsh and mire, a man alone,

full of care lest to his cost he never should

see the service of that Sire, that on that self night,

of a bright maid was born, our burden to quell.

And therefore sighing he said; 'I beseech thee, Lord,

and Mary, that is mildest mother so dear,

of some harbour where highly I might hear Mass,

and thy Matins tomorrow, meekly I ask,

and thereto promptly I pray my Pater and Ave

and Creed.'

He rode as he prayed,

And cried for his misdeeds;

He crossed himself always,

And said: 'Christ's Cross me speed!'

33

ow he had signed himself times but three,
when he was aware in the wood of a wall in a moat,
above a level, on high land locked under boughs
of many broad set boles about by the ditches:
a castle the comeliest that ever knight owned,
perched on a plain, a park all about,
with a pointed palisade, planted full thick,
encircling many trees in more than two miles.
The hold on the one side the knight assessed,
as it shimmered and shone through the shining oaks.
Then humbly has off with his helm, highly he thanks
Jesus and Saint Julian, that gentle are both,
that courtesy had him shown, and his cry hearkened.
'Now hospitality,' he said, 'I beseech you grant!'
Then goads he on Gringolet, with his gilded heels,
and he by chance there has chosen the chief way,
that brought the man bravely to the bridge's end
       in haste.
    The drawbridge was upraised,
    the gates were firm and fast,
    the walls were well arrayed –
    it trembled at no wind's blast.

'*A castle the comeliest that ever knight owned*'
Élaine (1867)
Baron Alfred Tennyson (1809-1892), Gustave Doré (1832-1883)

34

he knight stuck to his steed, that hugged the bank,

of the deep double ditch driven round the place.

The wall washed in the water wonderfully deep,

and then a full huge height it haled up aloft,

of hard hewn stone to the entablature,

embedded under the battlements in best style;

and there were turrets full tall towering between,

with many lovely loopholes clean interlocked:

a better barbican that knight never beheld.

And innermost he beheld a hall full high,

towers trim between, crenellated full thick,

fair finials that fused, and fancifully long,

with carven copes, cunningly worked.

Chalk white chimneys he descried enough,

on tower rooftops that gleamed full white.

So many painted pinnacles powdered there

among castle crenellations, clustered so thick,

that pared out of paper purely it seemed.

the fair knight on the horse it fine enough thought,

if he might contrive to come the cloister within,

to harbour in that hostel while Holy Day lasted,

      all content.

    He called and soon there came

    a porter pure pleasant.

    From the wall his errand he craved,

    and hailed the knight errant.

35

'ood sir,' quoth Gawain, 'will you do my errand

to the high lord of this house, harbour to crave?'

'Yes, by Saint Peter,' quoth the porter, 'for I believe

That you'll be welcome to dwell as long as you like.'

Then the welcomer on the wall went down swiftly,

and folk freely him with, to welcome the knight.

They let down the great drawbridge and dignified

knelt down on their knees upon the cold earth

to welcome this knight as they thought the worthiest way.

They yielded him the broad gate, opened wide,

and he them raised rightly and rode over the bridge.

Several then seized his saddle, while he alighted,

and then strong men enough stabled his steed.

Knights and their squires came down then

for to bring this bold man blithely to hall,

When he lifted his helmet, they hastened forward

to heft it from his hand, the guest to serve;

his blade and his blazon both they took.

then hailed he full handily the host each one,

and many proud men pressed close, that prince to honour.

All clasped in his noble armour to hall they him brought,

where a fair fire on a hearth fiercely flamed.

Then the lord of that land left his chamber

for to meet with manners the man on the floor.

He said: 'You are welcome to dwell as you like.

What is here, is all your own, to have at your will

and wield you.

'*Graunt merci,*' quoth Gawain,

'May Christ reward it you.'

As friends that meet again

Each clasped the other true.

36

awain gazed on the gallant that goodly him greet,
and thought him a brave baron that the burg owned,
a huge man in truth, and mature in his years;
broad, bright was his beard and all beaver-hued,
stern, striding strongly on stalwart shanks,
face fell as the fire, and free of his speech;
and well he seemed to suit, as the knight thought,
the leading a lordship, along of lords full good.
The chief him led to a chamber, expressly commands
a lord be delivered to him, him humbly to serve;
and there were brave for his bidding a band of men,
that brought him to a bright bower, the bedding was noble,
of curtains of clear silk with clean gold hems,
and coverlets full curious with comely panels,
of bright ermine above embroidered sides,
curtains running on cords, red gold rings,
tapestries tied to the wall, of Toulouse, Turkestan,
and underfoot, on the floor, that followed suit.
There he was disrobed, with speeches of mirth,
the burden of his mail and his bright clothes.
Rich robes full readily retainers brought him,
to check and to change and choose of the best.
Soon as he held one, and hastened therein,
that sat on him seemly, with spreading skirts,
verdant in his visage Spring verily seemed
to well nigh everyone, in all its hues,
glowing and lovely, all his limbs under,
that a comelier knight never Christ made,

they thought.

However he came here,

it seemed that he ought

to be prince without peer

on fields where fell men fought.

'A huge man in truth, and mature in his years'
Idylls of the King (p61, 1898)
Baron Alfred Tennyson (1809-1892), George Woolliscroft Rhead
(1854-1920), Louis Rhead (1857-1926)
The British Library

37

chair before the chimney, where charcoal burned,
graciously set for Gawain, was gracefully adorned,
coverings on quilted cushions, cunningly crafted both.
And then a mighty mantle was on that man cast
of a brown silk, embroidered full rich,
and fair furred within with pelts of the best –
the finest ermine on earth – his hood of the same.
And he sat on that settle seemly and rich,
and chafed himself closely, and then his cheer mended.
Straightway a table on trestles was set up full fair,
clad with a clean cloth that clear white showed,
the salt-cellars, napkins and silvered spoons.
The knight washed at his will, and went to his meat.
Servants him served seemly enough
with several soups, seasoned of the best,
double bowlfuls, as fitting, and all kinds of fish,
some baked in bread, some browned on the coals,
some seethed, some in stews savoured with spices,
and sauces ever so subtle that the knight liked.
While he called it a feast full freely and oft
most politely, at which all spurred him on politely
again:
'This penance now you take,
after it shall amend.'
That man much mirth did make,
for the wine to his head did tend.

'The knight washed at his will, and went to his meat'
The Romance of King Arthur and his Knights of the Round
Table (p290, 1917)
Sir Thomas Malory (15th cent), Alfred William Pollard (1859-
1944), Arthur Rackham (1867-1939)
Internet Archive Book Images

38

hen they sparred and parried in precious style
with private points put to the prince himself,
so he conceded courteously of that court he came,
where noble Arthur is headman himself alone,
that is the right royal king of the Round Table;
and that it is Gawain himself that in that house sits,
come there at Christmas, as chance has him driven.
When the lord learned what prince that he there had,
loud laughed he thereat, so delightful he thought it,
and all the men in that manse made it a joy
to appear in his presence promptly that time,
who all prize and prowess and purest ways
appends to his person, and praised is ever;
above all men upon earth his honour is most.
Each man full softly said to his neighbour:
'Now shall we see show of seemliest manners
and the faultless phrases of noble speaking.
What superior speech is, unasked we shall learn,
since we have found this fine master of breeding.
God has given us of his goodly grace forsooth,
that such a guest as Gawain grants us to have,
when barons blithe at His birth shall sit
      and sing.
    The meaning of manners here
    this knight now shall us bring.
    I hope whoever may hear
    Shall learn of love-making.'

39

hen the dinner was done and the diners risen,

it was nigh on the night that the time was near.

Chaplains to the chapel took their course,

ringing all men, richly, as they rightly should,

to the holy evensong of that high eventide.

The lord goes thereto and the lady as well;

into a comely enclosure quietly she enters.

Gawain gaily goes forth and thither goes soon;

the lord grasps him by the gown and leads him to sit,

acknowledges him with grace, calls him by name,

and said he was the most welcome man in the world;

and he thanked him thoroughly, they clasped each other,

and sat with sober seeming the service through.

Then liked the lady to look on the knight;

and came from the close with many fine women.

She was the fairest in feature, in flesh and complexion,

and in compass and colour and ways, of all others,

and fairer than Guinevere, as the knight thought.

He strode through the chancel to squire the dame.

Another lady her led by the left hand,

who was older than her, and aged it seemed,

and highly honoured with her men about her.

Not alike though to look on those ladies were,

for if the one was fresh, the other was withered:

rich red in this one distinguished her,

rough wrinkled cheeks on that other, in rolls.

Kerchiefs on this one, with many clear pearls,

her breast and her bright throat bare displayed

shone sweeter than snow that's shed on the hills;

that other swathed with a wimple wound at the throat,

clothed to her swarthy chin with chalk-white veils,

her forehead folded in silk, enveloped everywhere,

ringed and trellised with trefoils about,

that naught was bare of the lady but the black brows,

the two eyen and nose, the naked lips,

and those were sorry to see, and somewhat bleary –

a great lady on earth a man might her call,

      by God!

    Her body was short and thick,

    her buttocks big and broad;

    Much sweeter a sweet to lick

    the one at her side for sure.

'*She was the fairest in feature*'
Idylls of the King (p156, 1913)
Baron Alfred Tennyson (1809-1892), Eleanor Fortescue-
Brickdale (1872-1945)
The Internet Archive

40

hen Gawain gazed on that gracious-looking girl,

with leave asked of the lord he went to meet them.

The elder he hails, bowing to her full low;

the lovely-looking he laps a little in his arms,

he kisses her courteously and nobly he speaks.

They crave his acquaintance, and he quickly asks

to be their sworn servant, if they themselves wished.

They take him between them, and talking they lead him

to a chamber, to the chimney, and firstly they ask for

spices, which men unstintingly hastened to bring,

and the winning wine with them, every time.

The lord laughing aloft leaps full oft,

minding that mirth be made and many a time,

nobly lifted his hood, and on a spear hung it,

and wished him to win the worth and honour thereof

who most mirth might move at that Christmastide.

'And I shall swear, by my faith, to strive with the best

before I lose the hood, with the help of my friends.'

Thus with laughing words the lord makes all merry,

for to gladden Sir Gawain with games in the hall

>   that night.

>   Till, when it was time,

>   the lord demanded light.

>   Gawain his way did find

>   To bed as best he might.

41

n the morn, when each man minds that time

the dear Lord for our destiny to die was born,

joy waxes in each house in the world for His sake.

So did it there on that day with dainties many:

both when major and minor meals were eaten

deft men on the dais served of the best.

The old ancient wife highest she sits;

the lord, so I believe, politely beside her.

Gawain and the sweet lady together they sat

in the midst, as the masses came together;

and then throughout the hall, as seemed right,

each man in his degree was graciously served.

There was meat, there was mirth, there was much joy,

that it would be a trouble for me to tell all,

and however perchance I pined to make my point.

But yet I know Gawain and the sweet lady

such comfort of their company caught together

through their dear dalliance of courtly words,

with clean courteous chat, closed from filth,

their play surpassed every princely game with which it

compares.

Kettledrums and trumpets,

much piping there of airs;

Each man minded his,

and those two minded theirs.

42

uch mirth was there driven that day and another,

and a third as thickly thronged came in thereafter;

The joy of St John's Day was gentle to hear,

and was the last of the larking, the lords thought.

There were guests set to go on the grey morn,

so they stayed wonderfully waking and wine drank,

dancing the day in with noble carols.

At the last, when it was time, they took their leave,

each one to wend on his way into strange parts.

Gawain gave them good day, the good man grasps him,

and leads him to his own chamber, the chimney beside,

and there he grips him tight, heartily thanks him

for the fine favour that he had shown him,

so to honour his house on that Christmastide,

and embellish his burg with his bright cheer.

'Indeed, sir, while I live, I am the better

for Gawain being my guest at God's own feast.'

'Graunt merci, sir,' quoth Gawain, 'in good faith it's yours,

all the honour is your own – the High King requite you!

And I am here, at your will, to work your behest,

as I am beholden to do, in high things and low,

       by right.'

    The lord was at great pains

    To keep longer the knight;

    To him answers Gawain

    That by no means he might.

43

hen the lord aimed full fair at him, asking

what daring deed had him driven at that dear time

so keenly from the king's court to stray all alone,

before the holy holiday was haled out of town.

'Forsooth, sir,' quoth the knight, 'you say but the truth,

a high errand and a hasty had me from those halls,

for I am summoned myself to seek for a place,

with no thought in the world where to go find it.

I would not dare fail find it by New Year's morning

for all the land in Logres, so me our Lord help!

So, sir, this request I make of you here,

that you tell me true if ever you tale heard

of the green chapel, on what ground it stands,

and of the knight that keeps it, the colour of green.

There was established by statute a pact us between

both to meet at that mark, if I should live;

and of that same New Year but little is wanting,

and I would look on that lord, if God would let me,

more gladly, by God's Son, than any goods gain.

So, indeed, by your leave, it behoves me to go.

Now to work this business I've barely three days,

and it's fitter I fall dead than fail of my errand.'

Then, laughing, quoth the lord: 'Now stay, it behoves you,

for I'll teach you the trysting place ere the term's end.

The green chapel upon ground grieve for no more;

but you shall be in your bed, sir, at your ease,

while day unfolds, and go forth on the first of the year,

and come to that mark at mid-morn, to act as you wish

 and when.

 Dwell until New Year's Day,

 and rise and ride on then.

 You shall be shown the way;

 it is not two miles hence.'

44

hen was Gawain full glad, and gleefully he laughed:

'Now I thank you thoroughly beyond all things;

now achieved is my goal, I shall at your will

dwell here, and do what else you deem fit.'

Then the lord seized him and set him beside,

and the ladies had fetched, to please him the better.

There was seemly solace by themselves still.

The lord lofted for love notes so merry,

as one that wanted his wits, nor knew what he did.

Then he cried to the knight, calling aloud:

'You have deemed to do the deed that I bid.

Will you hold to this promise here and now?'

'Yes, sire, indeed,' said the knight and true,

'While I bide in your burg, I'm at your behest.'

'As you have travelled,' quoth the lord, 'from afar,

and since then waked with me, you are not well served

neither of sustenance nor of sleep, surely I know.

You shall linger in your room and lie there at ease

tomorrow till Mass, and then to meat wend

when you will, with my wife, that with you shall sit

and comfort you with company, till I come to court:

time spend,

And I shall early rise;

a-hunting will I wend.'

Gawain thinks it wise,

as is fitting to him bends.

45

nd further,' quoth the lord, 'a bargain we'll make:

whatsoever I win in the wood is worthily yours;

and whatever here you achieve, exchange me for it.

Sweet sir, swap we so – swear it in truth –

whether, lord, that way lies worse or better.'

'By God,' quoth Gawain the good, 'I grant it you,

and that you lust for to play, like it methinks.'

'Who'll bring us a beverage, this bargain to make?'

so said the lord of that land. They laughed each one,

they drank and dallied and dealt in trifles,

these lords and ladies, as long as they liked;

and then with Frankish faring, full of fair words,

they stopped and stood and softly spoke,

kissing full comely and taking their leave.

By many lively servants with flaming torches,

each brave man was brought to his bed at last

　　　full soft.

　　To bed yet ere they sped,

　　repeating the contract oft;

　　the old lord of that spread

　　could keep a game aloft.

PART III

46

ull early before the day the folk were risen;
Guests who would go their grooms they called on,
and they busied them briskly the beasts to saddle,
tightening their tackle, trussing their baggage.
The richest ready themselves to ride all arrayed,
leaping up lightly, latched onto their bridles,
each rode out by the way that he most liked.
The beloved lord of the land was not the last
arrayed for the riding, with ranks full many;
ate a sop hastily, when he had heard Mass,
with horns to the hunting field he hastens away.
By the time that daylight gleamed upon earth,
he with his knights on high horses were.
Then the cunning hunters coupled their hounds,
unclosed the kennel door and called them out,
blew briskly on their bugles three bare notes;
braches bayed therefore, and bold noise made,
and men chastised and turned those that chasing went,
a hundred of hunters, as I have heard tell,
            of the best.
      To station, keepers strode,
      huntsmen leashes off-cast;
      great rumpus in that wood
      there rose with their good blasts.

'*Then the cunning hunters coupled their hounds*'
Élaine (1867)
Baron Alfred Tennyson (1809-1892), Gustave Doré (1832-1883)

47

t the first call of the quest quaked the wild;
deer drove for the dales, darting for dread,
hied to the high ground, but swiftly they were
stayed by the beaters, with their stout cries.
They let the harts with high branched heads have way,
the brave bucks also with their broad antlers;
for the noble lord had bidden that in close season
no man there should meddle with those male deer.
The hinds were held back with a 'Hey' and a 'Ware!'
The does driven with great din to the deep coves.
There might men see, as they loosed, the slanting of arrows;
at each winding of the wood whistled a flight,
that bit into brown flanks, with broad blade-heads.
What screaming and bleeding, by banks they lay dying,
and ever the hounds in a rush hard on them followed,
hunters with high horn-calls hastened them after,
with such a crack and cry as cliffs were bursting.
What wild beasts so escaped the men shooting
were all dragged down and rent by the new reserves,
when hunted from high ground, and harried to water.
The lads were so skilled at the lower stations,
and the greyhounds so great, that gripped so quickly
and dragged them down, as swift I swear,

as sight.
In bliss without alloy
the lord does spur or alight,
and passes that day with joy
and so to the dark night.

'*At the first call of the quest quaked the wild*'
Viviane (1868)
Baron Alfred Tennyson (1809-1892), Gustave Doré (1832-1883)

48

hus larks the lord by linden-wood eaves,

while Gawain the good man gaily abed lies,

lurks till the daylight gleams on the walls,

under canopy full clear, curtained about.

And as in slumber he lay, softly he heard

a little sound at his door, and it slid open;

and he heaves up his head out of the clothes,

a corner of the curtain he caught up a little,

and watches warily to make out what it might be.

It was the lady, the loveliest to behold,

that drew the door after her full silent and still,

and bent her way to the bed; and the knight ashamed,

laid him down again lightly and feigned to sleep.

And she stepped silently and stole to his bed,

caught up the curtain and crept within,

and sat her full softly on the bedside

and lingered there long, to look when he wakened.

The lord lay low, lurked a full long while,

compassing in his conscience what this case might

mean or amount to, marvelling in thought.

But yet he said to himself: 'More seemly it were

to descry with speech, in a space, what she wishes.'

Then he wakened and wriggled and to her he turned,

and lifted his eyelids and let on he was startled,

and signed himself with his hand, as with prayer, to be

safer.

With chin and cheek full sweet,

both white and red together,

full graciously did she greet,

lips light with laughter.

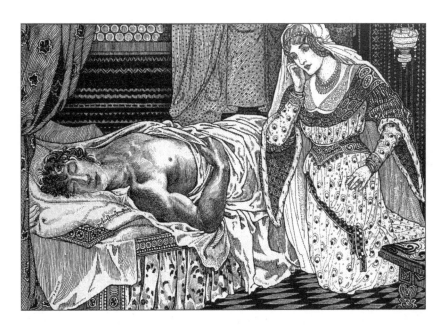

'*She stepped silently and stole to his bed*'
Idylls of the King (p19, 1898)
Baron Alfred Tennyson (1809-1892), George Woolliscroft Rhead
(1854-1920), Louis Rhead (1857–1926)
The British Library

49

'ood morning, Sir Gawain,' said that sweet lady,

'You are a sleeper unsafe, that one may slip hither.

Now are you taken in a trice, lest a truce we shape,

I shall bind you in your bed, that you may trust.'

All laughing the lady made her light jests.

'Good morrow, sweet,' quoth Gawain the blithe,

'I shall work your will, and that I well like,

for I yield me swiftly and sue for grace;

and that is the best, to my mind, since behoves I must.'

And thus he jested again with much blithe laughter.

'But would you, lovely lady, but grant me leave

and release your prisoner and pray him to rise,

I would bound from this bed and dress me better,

I should discover more comfort in speaking with you.'

'Nay, forsooth, beau sire,' said that sweet,

'You shall not rise from your bed. I charge you better:

I shall wrap you up here on this other side,

and then chat with my knight whom I have caught;

for I know well, indeed, Sir Gawain you are,

that all the world worships, wherever you ride.

Your honour, your courtesy, is nobly praised

among lords, among ladies, all who life bear.

And now you are here, indeed, and we on our own;

my lord and his lords are far off faring,

other knights are abed, and my ladies also,

the door drawn and shut with a strong hasp.

And since I have in this house him who all like,

I shall work my time well, while it lasts,

        with a tale.

    Your are welcome to my body,

    Your pleasure to take all;

    I must by necessity

    your servant be, and shall.'

50

'n good faith,' quoth Gawain, 'a gain's that me thinks,
though I be not now him of whom you are speaking;
to reach to such reverence as you rehearse here,
I am all ways unworthy, I know well myself.
By God, I'd be glad though if you thought it fit
in speech or service that I might set myself
to the pleasing of your worth – that were a pure joy.'
'In good faith, Sir Gawain,' quoth the sweet lady,
'The worth and the prowess that pleases all others,
if I slighted or thought light of it, that were little grace;
but there are ladies enough that would far rather
have you, dear man, to hold, as I have you here,
to dally dearly in your delightful words,
comfort themselves and ease their cares,
than make much of the treasure and gold they have.
But as I love that same Lord that the heavens rules,
I have wholly in my hand what all desire

        through grace.'
She made him thus sweet cheer,
who was so fair of face;
the knight with speeches clear
answered her every case.

51

'adam,' quoth the merry man, 'Mary give you grace,

for I have found, in good faith, your friendship is noble.

Others gain full much of other folks praise for their deeds,

but the deference they deal me is undeserved in my case.

It is honour to you that naught but good you perceive.'

'By Mary,' quoth the lady, 'methinks it otherwise;

for were I worth all the wonder of women alive,

and all the wealth of the world were in my hand,

and I should bargain to win myself a brave lord,

with the qualities that I know of you, knight, here,

of beauty and debonair and blithe seeming,

that I hearkened to ere now and have here found true,

then should no errant on earth before you be chosen.'

'Indeed, lady,' quoth the knight, 'you have done much better;

but I am proud of the value you place on me,

and, solemnly your servant, my sovereign I hold you,

and your knight I become, and Christ reward you!'

Thus they mulled many matters till mid-morn passed,

and ever the lady let fall that she loved him much;

yet the knight held to his guard, and acted full fair.

'Though I were loveliest lady,' so her mind had it,

'the less is there love in his load' – for his fate he sought

   that one,

  the stroke that should him cleave,

  and it must needs be done.

  The lady then sought to leave,

  he granting her that boon.

52

hen she gave him good day, with a laughing glance,
and stunned him as she stood there, with cutting words:
'May He who speeds each speech reward you this sport!
But that you should be Gawain, it baffles the mind.'
'Wherefore?' quoth the knight, and urgently asked,
fearful lest he had failed in forms of politeness.
But the lady blessed him and spoke as follows:
'One gracious as Gawain is rightly held to be,
with courtesy contained so clear in himself,
could not lightly have lingered so long with a lady,
but he had craved a kiss out of courtesy,
with some trifling touch at some tale's end.'
Then quoth Gawain: 'Indeed, let it be as you like;
I shall kiss at your command, as befits a knight,
and further, lest I displease you, so plead no more.'
She comes nearer at that, and catches him in her arms,
leans lovingly down, and the lord kisses.
They graciously commend to Christ one another;
and she goes out at the door with not a word more;
And he readies himself to rise and hurries anon,
calls to his chamberlain, chooses his clothes,
going forth, when he is ready, blithely to Mass.
And then he went to the noble meal that awaited,
and made merry all day till the moonrise,

       at games.
    Was never knight fairer sung
    between two such noble dames,
    the elder and the young;
    much joy had they of the same.

'*She comes nearer at that, and catches him in her arms*'
Idylls of the King (p220, 1913)
Baron Alfred Tennyson (1809-1892), Eleanor Fortescue-
Brickdale (1872-1945)
The Internet Archive

53

nd ever the lord of the land intent on his games,

hunted, in holts and heath, for barren hinds,

Such a sum he there slew by the set of sun,

of does and other deer, it were deemed a wonder.

Then fiercely they flocked in, folk at the last,

and quickly of the quenched deer a heap they made.

The noblest sped there with servants enough,

gathered the quarry greatest in flesh that were there,

and had them deftly undone as custom demands.

Some that were there searched them in assay,

and two fingers of fat they found on the feeblest.

Then they slit the slot, and seized the first stomach,

shaved it with sharp knives, and knotted the sheared.

Then lopped off the four limbs and rent off the hide,

next broke they the belly, the bowels out-taking,

deftly, lest they undid and destroyed the knot.

They gripped the gullet, and swiftly severed

the weasand from the windpipe and whipped out the guts.

Then sheared out the shoulders with their sharp knives,

hauled them through a little hole, left the sides whole.

Then they slit up the breast and broke it in twain.

And again at the gullet one then began

rending all readily right to the fork,

voiding the entrails, and verily thereafter

all the membranes by the ribs readily loosened.

So too they cleared to the backbone, rightly,

even down to the haunch that hangs from the same,

and heaved it all up whole and hewed it off there.

and that they properly call the *numbles*, I deem,

        by kind.

      At the fork then of the thighs

      they loose the lappets behind;

      to hew it in two they hie,

      by the backbone it to unbind.

54

oth the head and the neck they hewed off then,

and after sundered the sides swift from the chine,

and the ravens' fee they cast into a grove.

Then they skewered each thick flank by the ribs,

and hung each up by the hocks of the haunches,

every fellow taking his fee as it fell to him.

On a skin of the fair beast fed they their hounds

with the liver and lights, and the stomach lining,

and bread bathed in blood blent there among.

Boldly they blew the kill their hounds a-baying;

then rode home with the flesh tightly packed,

stalwartly sounding out many stout notes.

As the daylight was done, the company came

to the comely castle, where our knight bides

      all still,

    in bliss by bright fire set.

    The lord is come from the hill;

    when Gawain with him is met,

    there they but joy as they will.

55

hen the lord commanded all be summoned to the hall,

both the ladies, aloft, to descend with their maids.

Before all the folk on the floor, he bid men

verily his venison to bring there before him;

and all gaily in courtesy Gawain he called,

and tells over the tally of full fat beasts,

shows him the fine flesh shorn from the ribs.

'How does this sport please you? Have I won praise?

Have I won thanks, thoroughly served by my craft?'

'Yes, indeed,' quoth the other, 'here spoils are fairest

of all I have seen this seven-year in season of winter.'

'And I give all this to you, Gawain,' quoth the man then,

'for according to covenant you may call it your own.'

'That is so,' quoth the knight, 'I say you the same:

what I have worthily won this house within,

shall with as good a will be worthily yours.'

And he clasps his fair neck his arms within,

and kisses him in as comely a way as he can:

'Take you there my prize, I received no more;

I would grant it all, though it were greater.'

'That is good,' quoth the lord, 'many thanks therefore.

This may be the better gift, if you would tell me

where you won this same prize by your own wits.'

'That was not pledged,' quoth he, 'ask me no more;

for you have taken what's due, none other to you

I owe.'
They laughed and made blithe
with words worth praise, and so
to supper then side by side,
with dainties in plenty go.

'*Then the lord commanded all be summoned to the hall*'
Élaine (1867)
Baron Alfred Tennyson (1809-1892), Gustave Doré (1832-1883)

56

nd then by the chimney in chamber sitting,

servants brought to them choice wines oft,

and in their banter they agreed in that morn

to fulfil the same bond they had made before:

what chance might betide, their prize to exchange,

each new thing they named, at night when they met.

They made accord of this covenant before all the court;

and beverage was brought forth in banter at this time.

Then they lovingly took their leave at the last,

each man at his leaving going brisk to his bed.

When the cock had crowed and cackled but thrice,

the lord leapt from his bed, the liegemen each one,

so that meat and a Mass were swiftly delivered,

the company off to the wood, ere daylight sprang,

      to the chase.

   Proudly with huntsmen and horns

   through wilds they passed apace,

   uncoupled among the thorns,

   the hounds ran headlong race.

57

oon they called for a search by the marsh-side,
the huntsman urged on the first hounds up,
wild cries he uttered with wondrous noise.
The hounds that heard him hastened there swiftly,
and fell as fast to the trail, forty at once.
Then such a baying and clamour of gathered hounds
rose that the rocks rang out all about.
Huntsmen harried them with horn and by mouth;
then all in a pack they swung together
between a pool in that place and a cruel crag.
On a knoll by a cliff, at the marsh side,
where the rough rock had ruggedly fallen,
they sped to the finding, the huntsmen after.
They surrounded the crag and the knoll both,
while they made sure they had well within
the beast that was bayed at, there, by their bloodhounds.
Then they beat at the bushes and bade him rise up,
and he savagely swung athwart the huntsmen –
a most splendid boar it was, rushed out there,
solitary through age, long split from the herd,
but he was still mighty, the greatest of boars,
full grim when he grunted. Then grieved many
for three hounds at first thrust he felled to the earth,
and sped him forth at great speed all unscathed.
The hunt hallooed 'Hi!' full loud, and cried 'Hey! Hey!

and horns to mouths, hastily recalled them.

Many were the merry cries of men and of hounds

that brisk chased the boar, with barking and clamour,

      to quell,

    Full oft he bides at bay

    and downs the dogs pell-mell;

    he harries the hounds, and they

    full piteously yowl and yell.

58

 haping to shoot him some shoved through then,

hurling their arrows at him, hitting him often;

but their points were parried by bristling flanks,

and their barbs would not bite there in his brow,

though the smooth shaft were shattered in pieces,

the head skipped away wherever it hit.

but when by dint of dire strokes they damaged him,

then, maddened by baiting, he rushes the men,

hurts them full heavily as forth he hies,

and many were awed at that and drew backwards.

But the lord on a lithe horse lunges after him,

as knight bold in the battle his bugle he blows,

rallied the hounds as he rode through rank thicket,

pursuing this wild swine till the sun had set.

The day with these same deeds they passed in this wise,

while our courteous knight lay in his bed,

Gawain gladly at home, in gear full rich

of hue.

The lady did not forget,

to come to greet him too;

full early she him beset

to seek a change of mood.

'*Hurling their arrows at him, hitting him often*'
The Romance of King Arthur and his Knights of the Round
Table (p518, 1917)
Sir Thomas Malory (15th cent), Alfred William Pollard (1859-
1944), Arthur Rackham (1867-1939)
Internet Archive Book Images

59

 he came to the curtain and peeped at the knight.

Sir Gawain welcomed her courteously first,

and she answered him again eager her words,

sits herself soft by his side, and sweetly she laughs,

and with a loving look she led with these words:

'Sir, if you be Gawain, it's a wonder methinks,

why one so well disposed always to good,

knows not how to manage his manners in company,

and if any teach you to know them, you cast them from mind.

You have swiftly forgot what but yesterday I taught

with all the truest tokens of talk that I could.'

'What is that?' quoth the knight, 'Indeed I know not.

If it be truth that you breathe, the blame is mine own.'

'Yet I taught you of kissing.' quoth the fair dame,

'where countenance is fair, quick make your claim;

that becomes every knight that courtesy uses.'

'Unsay,' quoth that brave man, 'my dear, that speech,

for that I dare not do, lest I were denied;

if I were spurned, I'd be wrong, indeed, to have proffered.'

'By my faith,' quoth the lady, 'you cannot be spurned;

you are strong enough to constrain by strength, if you like,

if any were so villainous as to deny you.'

'Yes, by God,' quoth Gawain, 'true is your speech,

but threats do never thrive in the land where I live,

nor any gift that is given without a good will.

I am at your command, to kiss when you like;

you may lip when you will, and leave when you wish

in a space.'
The lady bends her adown
and sweetly she kisses his face;
much speech they there expound
of love, its grief and grace.

60

'would know of you, knight,' that lady then said,

'if you are not angered by this, what is the reason

that so young and lively a one as you at this time,

so courteous, so knightly, as widely you're known

(and from all chivalry to choose, the chief things praised

are the laws of loyal love, and the lore of arms;

for in telling those tales of the truest of knights,

all the title and text of their works is taken

from how lords hazard their lives for loyal love,

endured for that duty's sake dreadful trials,

and after with valour avenged, and void their cares,

brought bliss to the bower by bounties their own)

and you, the knight, the noblest child of your age,

your high fame and honour told everywhere,

why I have sat by yourself here separately twice,

yet heard I never that your head held even a word

that ever belonged to love, the less nor the more.

And you, that are so courteous and coy of your vows,

ought, to a young thing, to yearn to show

and teach some tokens of true love's craft

What! Are you ignorant, who garner all praise,

or else do you deem me too dull to heed your dalliance?

For shame!

I come hither single and sit

to learn of you some game;

do teach me of your wit,

while my lord is away.'

61

'In good faith,' quoth Gawain, 'may God reward you!

Great is the gladness, and pleasure to me,

that so worthy as you should wind her way hither,

at pains with so poor a man as to sport with your knight

with any show of favour – it sets me at ease.

But to take on the travail myself of expounding true love,

and touch on the themes of the texts and tales of arms

to you who, I know well, wield more skill

in that art, by half, than a hundred of such

as I am or ever shall be, on this earth where I live –

that were a manifold folly, my dear, by my troth.

I would your wishes work if ever I might,

as I am highly beholden, and evermore will

be servant to yourself, so save me God!'

Thus that lady framed her questions and tempted him oft,

for to win him to woe, whatever else she thought of;

but he defended himself so fairly no fault it seemed,

no evil on either hand, nor did they know aught

        but bliss.

    They laughed and larked full long;

    at the last she did him kiss,

    farewell was on her tongue,

    and went her way, with this.

'*At the last she did him kiss*'
The Romance of King Arthur and his Knights of the Round
Table (p214, 1917)
Sir Thomas Malory (15th cent), Alfred William Pollard (1859-
1944), Arthur Rackham (1867-1939)
Internet Archive Book Images

62

hen bestirs him the knight and rises for Mass,
and then the dinner was done and duly served.
The knight with the ladies larked all day,
but the lord of the land gallops full oft,
hunts the ill-fated swine, that surges by banks
and bites the best of his hounds' backs asunder
biding at bay, till bowmen bettered him,
made him head for the open, for all he could do,
so fast flew the arrows where those folk gathered.
But yet at times the bravest he made to start,
till at the last so weary he was he could not run,
but, with best haste he might, to a hole he wins
in the bank, by a rock where runs the burn.
He got the bank at his back, began to scrape,
the froth foamed from his mouth foul at the corners,
and he whet his white tusks. It was irksome then
to the all the beaters so bold that by him stood
to harass him from afar, but nigh him no man
dared go.

He had hurt so many before
that all were then full loath
to be torn by his tusks once more,
that was fierce and frenzied both.

63

Till the lord came himself, urged on his horse,

saw the boar bide at bay, his men beside.

He alights lively adown, leaves his courser,

brings out a bright blade and boldly strides forth,

fast through the ford, where the fell foe bides.

The wild beast was wary of one with a weapon in hand,

his bristles rose high, so fiercely he snorts

that folk feared for the lord, lest worst him befell.

The swine straight away set on the man,

that the baron and boar were both in a heap,

in the white water. The worst had the creature,

For the man marked him well, as they first met,

set the sharp point firm in its chest-hollow,

hit him up to the hilt, so the heart burst asunder,

and he yielded him snarling, downstream was swept

       outright.

      A hundred hounds him rent,

      that bravely could him bite;

      beaters brought him to bank

      and the dogs to death, in fight.

64

here was blowing the kill on many brave horns,

halloing on high as loud as men might;

Hounds bayed at the beast, as bid by their masters,

who of that hard chase were the chief huntsmen.

Then a man who was wisest in woodcraft

with loving care to undo the beast begins:

first he hews off his head and sets it on high,

then rends him roughly along the ridge of his back,

brings out the bowels, and broils them on coals,

with bread blent therewith his hounds rewards.

Then he breaks out the brawn in broad bright slabs,

and has out the entrails, as is seemly and right;

attaches the two halves wholly together,

and then on a strong stake stoutly them hangs.

Now with this same swine they set off for home;

the boar's head was borne before the baron himself,

who felled him down by the ford through force of his hand

so strong.

Till he saw Sir Gawain

in the hall it seemed full long;

he calls, and he comes again

for the dues that to him belong.

65

he lord, full loud he cried, laughed merrily

when he saw Sir Gawain; and with joy he speaks.

The good ladies were summoned, the household gathered;

he shows him the boar's sides, and shapes him the tale

of the largeness and length, the malignity also,

of the war on the wild swine in woods where he fled.

So the other knight full nobly commended his deeds,

and praised it, the great merit that he had proved;

for such brawn from a beast, the brave knight said,

nor such flanks on a swine he'd not seen before.

Then they handled the huge head, the knight gave praise,

and showed horror at it, for the lord to hear.

'Now Gawain,' quoth the good man, 'this game is your own,

by a firm and fast promise, as in faith you know.'

'That is true,' quoth the knight, 'and as surely true

is that all I got I shall give you again, by my troth.'

He clasped the lord at the neck and gently kissed him,

and after that of the same he again served him there.

'Now are we even quit,' quoth the knight, 'this eventide,

of all the covenants made here, since I came hither,

     by law.'

    The lord said: 'By Saint Giles,

    you are the best that I know;

    you'll be rich in a while,

    if your trade continues so.'

66

hen they set up tables on trestles aloft,

casting cloths on them. Clear light then

wakened the walls, waxen torches

servants set, and served food all about.

Much gladness and glee gushed out therein

round the fire on the floor, and in fulsome wise

at the supper and after, many noble songs,

such as Christmas carols and dances new,

with all manner of mirth that man may tell of,

and ever our courteous knight the lady beside.

Such sweetness to that man she showed all seemly,

with secret stolen glances, that stalwart knight to please,

that all wondering was the man, and wrath with himself;

but he could not out of breeding spurn her advances,

but dealt with her daintily, howsoever the deed might

be cast.

When they had dallied in hall

as long as their will might last,

to chamber the lord him called,

and to the hearth they passed.

67

nd there they drank and debated and decided anew

to act on the same terms on New Year's Eve;

but the knight craved leave to go forth on the morn,

for it was nearing the time when he must go.

The lord persuaded him not to, pressed him to linger,

and said: 'As I am true, I pledge you my troth

you shall gain the Green Chapel, and render your dues,

sir, by New Year's light, long before prime.

And so go lie in your room and take your ease,

and I shall hunt in the holt and hold to the covenant,

exchanging what has chanced, when I spur hither;

for I have tested you twice, and faithful I find you.

Now: "third time pays all," think on that tomorrow;

Make we merry while we may, and mind only joy,

for a man may find sorrow whenever he likes.'

This was graciously granted and Gawain lingered;

Blithely they brought him drink, and bed-wards they went

      with light.

    Sir Gawain lies down and sleeps

    full still and soft all night;

    the lord who to woodcraft keeps,

    rises early and bright.

68

fter Mass a morsel he and his men took;

merry was the morning, his mount he summoned.

All the men that a-horse were followed him after,

ready set on their steeds before the hall gates.

Fairest of fair was the field, for the frost clung.

In red ruddiness on wrack rises the sun,

and, full clear, casts the clouds from the welkin.

Huntsmen unleashed the hounds by a holt side;

rocks in woods rang out with the cry of the horns.

some hounds fell to the track where the fox lurked,

oft traversing the trail by dint of their wiles.

A little one cried scent, the huntsman to him called;

his fellows fell to, panting full thick,

running forth in a rabble on the right track.

And fox frisked before them; they found him soon,

and when they had him in sight pursued him fast,

marking him clearly with wrathful noise;

and he twists and turns through many a tangled grove,

doubles back and hearkens by hedges full often.

At the last by a little ditch he leaps over a thicket,

steals out full silent by the side of a valley,

thinks to slip from the wood by guile, from the hounds.

Then he came, ere he knew it, to a fine hunt-station,

where three hounds in a cleft threaten him together,

all grey.
There he started aside
and boldly he did stray;
with all the woe in life,
to the wood he went away.

69

hen was it lively delight to list to the hounds,

when all the meet had met him, mingled together.

Such curses at that sight rained down on his head

as if all the clinging cliffs clattered down in a heap.

Here was he hallooed when huntsmen met him,

loud was he greeted with snarling speech;

there he was threatened and called thief often,

and ever the hounds at his tail, that he might not tarry.

Oft he was rushed at when he made for the open,

and often swerved back again, so wily was Reynard.

and so he led them astray, the lord and his liegemen,

in this manner by mountains till after mid-morning,

while the honoured knight at home happily slept

within the comely curtains, on that cold morn.

But the lady for love could get no sleep,

nor could the purpose impair pitched in her heart,

but rose up swiftly, and took herself thither

in a merry mantle, that reached the earth,

that was furred full fine with purest pelts;

without coif on her head, but the noblest gems

traced about her hair-net by twenties in clusters;

her fair face and her throat shown all naked,

her breast bare before, and her back the same.

She came in by the chamber door and closed it after,

threw open a window and to the knight called,

and roundly thus rebuked him with her rich words

with cheer:

'Ah! Man, how can you sleep?

This morning is so clear.'

He was in slumber deep,

and yet he could her hear.

70

n heavy depths of dreaming murmured that noble,

as one that was troubled with thronging thoughts,

of how destiny would that day deal him his fate

at the Green Chapel, where he must meet his man,

bound there to bear his buffet without more debate.

But when he had fully recovered his wits,

he started from dreaming and answered in haste.

The lovely lady with laughter so sweet,

bent over his fair face and fully him kissed.

He welcomed her worthily with noble cheer;

he saw her so glorious and gaily attired,

so faultless of feature and of such fine hue,

bright welling joy warmed all his heart.

With sweet smiling softly they slip into mirth,

that to all bliss and beauty, that breaks between them,

       they win.

    They spoke in words full good,

    much pleasure was therein;

    in great peril would have stood,

    kept not Mary her knight from sin.

71

or that peerless princess pressed him so closely,
urged him so near the edge, he felt it behoved him
either to bow to her love, or with loathing refuse her.

He cared for his courtesy, lest he were churlish,

and more for the mischief if he should work sin

and be traitor to that lord who held the dwelling.

'God shield us!' quoth the knight, 'that must not befall!'

With loving laughter a little he put aside

all the special pleading that sprang from her mouth.

Quoth beauty to the brave: 'Blame you deserve,

if you love not that live lady that you lie next,

who above all of the world is wounded in heart,

unless you have a leman, a lover, that you like better,

and firm of faith to that fair one, fastened so hard

that you list not to loose it – and that I believe.

If that you tell me that truly, I pray you;

by all the lovers alive, hide not the truth

　　　　with guile.'

　　　The knight said: 'By Saint John,'

　　　and gentle was his smile

　　　'In faith I love no one,

　　　nor none will love the while.'

72

hese words,' said the lady, 'are the worst words of all;

but I am answered forsooth, so that it grieves me.

Kiss me now gently, and I shall go hence;

I may but mourn upon earth, a maid that loves much.'

Sighing she stooped down, and sweetly him kissed,

and then she severs from him, and says as she stands:

'Now, dear, at this our parting set me at ease:

give me something, a gift, if only your glove,

that I may think of you, man, my mourning to lessen.'

'Now indeed,' quoth the knight, 'I would I had here

the dearest thing, for your sake, I own in the world,

for you have deserved, forsooth, and in excess,

a richer reward, by rights, than I might reckon;

but as a love-token, this would profit you little.

It is not to your honour to have at this time

a glove of Gawain's giving to treasure;

and I am here on an errand in lands unknown,

and have no servants with sacks of precious things.

I dislike this, my lady, for your sake, at this time;

but each man must do as he must, take it not ill

      nor pine.'

        'Nay, knight of high honours,'

        quoth that love-some lady fine,

        'though I shall have naught of yours,

        yet shall you have of mine.'

'Kiss me now gently, and I shall go hence'
The Boy's King Arthur (p130, 1922)
Sidney Lanier (1842-1881), Newell Convers Wyeth (1882-1945)
Wikimedia Commons

73

he proffered him a rich ring of red gold work,

with a sparkling stone glittering aloft,

that blazed brilliant beams like the bright sun;

know you well that it's worth was full huge.

But the knight refused it and he readily said:

'I'll no gifts, before God, my dear, at this time;

I have none to give you, nor naught will I take.'

She offered it him eagerly, yet he her gift spurned,

and swore swiftly his oath that he would not seize it;

and she grieved he refused her, and said thereafter:

'Since you reject my ring, too rich it may seem,

for you would not be so high beholden to me,

I shall give you my girdle: that profits you less.'

She loosed a belt lightly that lay round her sides,

looped over her kirtle beneath her bright mantle.

Gear it was of green silk and with gold trimmed,

at the edges embroidered, with finger-stitching;

and that she offered the knight, and blithely besought

that he would take it though it were unworthy.

but he said he might have nigh him in no wise

neither gold nor treasure, ere God sent him grace,

to achieve the errand he had chosen there.

'And therefore, I pray you, be not displeased,

and let your gift go, for I swear it I can never

> you grant.
> To you I am deeply beholden,
> your kindness is so pleasant,
> and ever in heat and cold, then
> I'll be your true servant.'

74

'ow do you shun this silk,' said the lady,

'because it is simple in itself? And so it may seem.

Lo! It is slight indeed, and so is less worthy.

But whoso knew the worth woven therein

he would hold it in higher praise, perchance;

for whatever man is girt with this green lace,

while he has it closely fastened about him,

there is no man under heaven might hew him,

for he may not be slain by any sleight upon earth.'

Then the knight thought, and it came to his heart,

it was a jewel for the jeopardy judged upon him,

when he gained the Green Chapel, his fate to find;

if he might slip past un-slain, the sleight were noble.

Then he indulged her suit, and told her to speak.

And she pressed the belt on him urging it eagerly;

and he granted it, and she gave it him with goodwill,

and besought him, for her sake, never to reveal it,

but loyally conceal it from her lord. The knight agrees

that no one should know of it, indeed, but they two,

betimes.

He thanked her as he might,

with all his heart and mind.

By then the gallant knight,

she had kissed three times.

75

 hen took she her leave and left him there,

for more of that man she might not get.

When she is gone, Sir Gawain attires himself,

rises and dresses himself in noble array,

lays aside the love-lace the lady gave him,

hides it full handily where he might find it.

Then swiftly to the chapel took he his way,

privately approached a priest, and there prayed him

that he would enlighten his life and teach him better

how his soul might be saved when he went hence.

Then he shrove himself fully, eschewed his misdeeds

the major and minor, and mercy beseeches,

and calls on the priest for absolution;

and he absolved him surely and left him so pure

that Doomsday yet might be declared on the morn.

And then he made himself merry among the fair ladies,

with comely carols and all manner of joy,

more than ever before that day, till the dark night,

in bliss.

Each one had courtesy there

of him, and said: 'He is

the merriest he was ever

since he came hither, ere this.'

76

ow long in that leisure there let him abide!

Yet is the lord on his land, pursuing his sport.

He has done for the fox that he followed so long.

As he spurred through a spinney to spy the shrew,

there where he heard the hounds harry him on,

Reynard came rushing through the rough grove,

and all the rabble in a race, right at his heels.

The lord, aware of the wild thing, warily waits,

and brandishes his bright blade, drives at the beast.

And it shunned the sharp edge and sought to retreat;

but a hound rushed at him, before ere he might,

and right before the horse's feet they fell on him all

and worried the wily one with a wrathful noise.

The lord swiftly alighted then and latched on,

raised him full suddenly out of the ravening mouths,

holds him high over his head, halloos full loud,

while there bayed at him many brave hounds.

Huntsmen hied them thither with horns full many,

sounding the rally aright till they saw their lord.

When his noble company had all come in,

all that ever bore bugle blew at once,

and all the others hallooed who had no horn.

It was the merriest meet that ever men heard,

the ripe roar raised there for Reynard's soul from every

man's throat.

Their hounds they then reward,

Their heads they fondle and stroke;

and then they take Reynard

and strip him of his coat.

77

nd then they hurry for home, for it was nigh night,

striking up strongly on their stout horns.

The lord alights at last at his much-loved home,

finds fire upon hearth, the knight there beside,

Sir Gawain the good who glad was withal –

for among the ladies he was joyfully beloved.

He wore a gown of blue that reached to the ground.

His surcoat suited him well, all soft with fur,

and his hood of the same hung from his shoulder,

trimmed all with ermine were both all about.

He met with the lord in the midst of the floor,

and all with joy did him greet, and gladly he said:

'I shall fulfil the first our contract now,

that we settled so speedily sparing no drink.'

Then he clasped the lord and kissed him thrice,

as strongly and steadily as he well could.

'By Christ,' quoth the other, 'you've found much luck

in transacting this trade, if your profit was good.'

'You need not care about profit,' quick quoth the other,

'as I've promptly paid over the profit I took.'

'Marry,' quoth the other, 'my own falls behind,

for I have hunted all this day, and naught have I got

but this foul fox fell – the fiend take such goods! –

and that's a poor price to pay for such precious things

as you so have given me here, three such kisses

    so good.'
'Enough,' quoth Sir Gawain,
'I thank you, by the Rood.'
And how the fox was slain
the lord told as they stood.

78

ith mirth and minstrelsy, with meals at will,

they made as merry as any men might,

with laughter of ladies, and jesting with words.

Gawain and the good man so glad are they both:

must be, lest the diners are drunkards or dotards.

Both master and men played many jokes,

till the time it was come that they must sever;

his men at the last must go to their beds.

Then humbly his leave of the lord at first

takes the noble knight, and fairly him thanks:

'For such a splendid sojourn as I have had here,

your honour at this high feast, the High King reward you!

I would give myself as one of your men, if you so like;

but I must needs, as you know, move on tomorrow,

if you'll grant me a guide to show, as you promised,

the way to the Green Chapel, as God wills for me

to be dealt on New Year's day the doom my fate brings.'

'In good faith,' quoth the good man, 'by my goodwill

all that ever I promised you, I shall hold ready.'

Then he assigned him a servant to show him the way

and conduct him through the hills, so he'd not delay,

and faring through forest and thickset the shortest way

      he'd weave.

    The lord Gawain did thank,

    such honour he did receive.

    Then of the ladies of rank

    the knight must take his leave.

79

ith sad care and kissing he spoke to them still,
and full heartfelt thanks he pressed on them:
and they yielded him again replies the same,
commending him to Christ then with frozen sighs.
So from the company he courteously parts;
each man that he met, he gave him his thanks
for his service and for the solicitous care
that they had shown busied about him in serving;
and all were as sorry to sever from him there
as if they had dwelt nobly with that knight ever.
Then the lads with lights led him to his chamber,
and blithely brought him to bed to be at his rest.
If he did not sleep soundly, I dare say nothing,
for he had much on the morrow to mind, if he would,

> in thought.
> Let him lie there quite still,
> he is near what he sought;
> and quiet you a while until
> I tell you of all that they wrought.

PART IV

80

ow nears the New Year and the night passes,

the day drives away dark, as the Deity bids.

But wild weather awoke in the world outside,

clouds cast cold keenly down to the earth,

with wind enough from the north, to flail the flesh.

The snow sleeted down sharp, and nipped the wild;

the whistling wind wailed from the heights

and drove each dale full of drifts full great.

The knight listened full well, as he lay in his bed.

Though he closes his lids, full little he sleeps;

with each cock that crew he well knew his tryst.

Deftly he dressed himself, ere the day sprang,

for there was a lighted lamp gleamed in his chamber.

He called to his servant who promptly replied,

and bade him bring coat of mail and saddle his mount;

the man rises up and fetches him his clothes,

and attires Sir Gawain in splendid style.

First he clad him in clothes to ward off the cold,

and then in his harness, that burnished was kept,

both his belly-armour and plate, polished full bright,

the rings of his rich mail-coat rubbed free of rust;

and all was as fresh as at first, and he to give thanks

was glad.

He had put on each piece

and in bright armour clad ;

fairest from here to Greece,

his steed to be brought he bade.

81

hile he wound himself in the most splendid weeds –

his coat-armour with its badge of clear deeds,

set out upon velvet, with virtuous stones

embellished and bound about it, embroidered seams,

and fair lined within with fine furs –

yet he forgot not the lace, the lady's gift;

that Gawain did not fail of, for his own good.

when he had bound the blade on his smooth haunches,

then he wound the love-token twice him about,

swiftly swathed it about his waist sweetly that knight.

The girdle of green silk that gallant well suited,

upon that royal red cloth that rich was to show.

But it was not for its richness he wore this girdle,

nor for pride in the pendants, though polished they were,

and though the glittering gold gleamed at the ends,

but to save himself when it behoved him to suffer,

to abide baneful stroke without battling with blade

      or knife.

    With that the knight all sound,

    goes swift to risk his life;

    all the men of renown

    he thanks, prepares for strife.

82

hen was Gringolet readied, that was huge and great,
and had been stabled snugly and in secure wise;
he was eager to gallop, that proud horse then.
The knight went to him and gazed at his coat,
and said soberly to himself, and swore by the truth:
'Here are many, in this motte, that of honour think.
The man who maintains it, joy may he have!
The fair lady through life may love her befall!
Thus if they for charity cherish a guest,
and hold honour in their hand, the Lord them reward
who upholds the heavens on high, and also you all!
And if I should live for any while upon earth,
I would grant you some reward readily, if I might.'
Then steps he into the stirrup and strides aloft.
His man showed him his shield; on shoulder he slung it,
gives spur to Gringolet with his gilded heels,
and he starts forth on the stones – pausing no longer

       to prance.
    His servant to horse got then,
    who bore his spear and lance.
    'This castle to Christ I commend:
    May he grant it good chance!'

Part IV

83

The drawbridge was let down, and the broad gates
unbarred and flung open upon both sides.
The knight blessed himself swiftly, and passed the boards;
praised the porter kneeling before the prince,
who gives him God and good-day, that Gawain He save;
and goes on his way with his one man,
who shall teach him the path to that perilous place
where the grievous blow he shall receive.
They brushed by banks where boughs were bare,
they climbed by cliffs where clung the cold.
the heavens were up high, but ugly there-under
mist moved on the moors, melted on mountains,
each hill had a hat, a mist-mantle huge.
Brooks boiled and broke their banks about,
sheer shattering on shores where they down-flowed.
Well wild was the way where they by woods rode,
till it was soon time that the sun in that season
       does rise.
    They were on a hill full high,
    the white snow lay beside;
    the man that rode him by
    bade his master abide.

84

'For I have brought you hither, sir, at this time,
and now you are not far from that noted place
that you have sought and spurred so specially after.
But I must say, forsooth, that since I know you,
and you are a lord full of life whom I well love,
if you would hark to my wit, you might do better.
The place that you pace to full perilous is held;
there lives a man in that waste, the worst upon earth,
for he is strong and stern and loves to strike,
and more man he is than any upon middle-earth,
and his body bigger than the best four
that are in Arthur's house, Hector, or others.
He makes it so to chance at the Green Chapel,
that none passes by that place so proud in arms
that he but does him to death by dint of his hand;
for he is a mighty man, and shows no mercy,
for be it churl or chaplain that rides by the chapel,
monk or priest of the Mass, or any man else,
he is as quick to kill him, as to live himself.
Therefore I say, as true as you sit in the saddle,
come there, and you will be killed, if he has his way,
trust me truly in that, though you had twenty lives
        to spend.
    He has lived here of yore,
    and battled to great extent.
    Against his blows full sore,
    you may not yourself defend.'

'The place that you pace to full perilous is held'
Énide (1867)
Baron Alfred Tennyson (1809-1892), Gustave Doré (1832-1883)

85

'herefore, good Sir Gawain, let him alone,

and go by some other way, for God's own sake!

Course some other country where Christ might you speed.

And I shall hie me home again, and undertake

that I shall swear by God and all his good saints –

so help me God and the Holy things, and oaths enough –

that I shall loyally keep your secret, and loose no tale

that ever you fled from any man that I know of.'

'Grant merci,' quoth Gawain, and galled he said:

'It is worthy of you, man, to wish for my good,

and loyally keep my secret I know that you would.

But, keep it ever so quiet, if I passed here,

and fled away in fear, in the form that you tell of,

I were a cowardly knight, I might not be excused.

For I will go to the chapel, whatever chance may befall,

and talk with that same fellow in whatever way I wish,

whether it's weal or woe, as fate may to me

      behave.

   Though he be a stern fellow

   to manage, armed with a stave,

   full well does the Lord know

   His servants how to save.'

86

arry!' quoth the other man, 'now you spell it out
that you will take all your own trouble on yourself,
if you will lose your life, I'll not you delay.
Have your helm here on your head, your spear in your hand,
and ride down this same track by yon rock side,
till you're brought to the bottom of the wild valley,
then look a little on the level, to your left hand,
and you shall see in that vale that selfsame chapel
and the burly giant on guard that it keeps.
Now farewell, in God's name, Gawain the noble!
For all the gold in the ground I'd not go with you,
nor bear fellowship through this forest one foot further.'
With that the man in the wood tugs at his bridle,
hits his horse with his heels as hard as he might,
leaps away over the land, and leaves the knight there
       alone.
    'By God's self,' quoth Gawain,
    'I will neither weep nor groan;
    to God's will I bend again
    and I am sworn as His own.'

87

 o he gives spur to Gringolet and picks up the path,
pushing on through, by a bank, at the side of a wood,
rode down the rough slope right to the dale.
And then he gazed all about, and wild it seemed,
and saw no sign of shelter anywhere near,
but high banks and steep upon either side,
and rough rugged crags with gnarled stones;
so the sky seemed to be grazed by their barbs.
Then he halted and reined in his horse awhile,
and scanned all about this chapel to find.
He saw no such thing either side, and thought it quite strange,
save a little mound, as it were, off in a field,
a bald barrow by a bank beside the burn,
by a force of the flood that flowed down there;
the burn bubbled therein as if it were boiling.
The knight urges on his mount and comes to the mound,
alights there lightly, and ties to a lime-tree
the reins of his horse round a rough branch.
Then he goes to the barrow, and about it he walked,
debating with himself what it might be.
It had a hole at each end and on either side,
and was overgrown with grass in great knots;
and all was hollow within, naught but an old cave,
or a crevice of an old crag – he could not distinguish
        it well.
    'Who knows, Lord,' quoth the gentle knight
    'whether this be the Green Chapel?
    Here might about midnight
    the Devil his Matins tell!'

'The knight urges on his mount and comes to the mound'
Stories of the Days of King Arthur (1882)
Charles Henry Hanson, Gustave Doré (1832-1883)

88

'N ow indeed,' quoth Gawain, 'desolation is here;
this oratory is ugly, with weeds overgrown;
well is it seemly for the man clad in green
to deal his devotion here in the devil's wise.
Now I feel it's the Fiend, in my five senses,
who set me this meeting to strike at me here.
This is a chapel of mischance – bad luck it betide!
It is the most cursed church that ever I came to.'
With high helm on his head, his lance in his hand,
he roamed up to the roof of that rough dwelling.
Then he heard from that high hill, from a hard rock
beyond the brook, on the bank, a wondrous brave noise.
What! It clanged through the cliff as if it would cleave it,
as if on a grindstone one ground a great scythe.
What! It whirred and whetted, as water in a mill.
What! It rushed and rang, revolting to hear.
Then 'By God,' quoth Gawain, 'this here I believe
is arranged to reverence me, to greet rank

     by rote.

  'Let God's will work! "Alas" –

will help me not a mote.

My life though it be lost

I dread no wondrous note.'

89

hen the knight called out loud on high;

'Who stands in this stead, my tryst to uphold?

For now is good Gawain grounded right here.

If any man wills aught, wind hither fast,

either now or never his needs to further.'

'Abide,' quoth one on the bank above his head,

'and you shall have all in haste I promised you once.'

Yet he then turned to his tumult swiftly a while,

and at whetting he worked, ere he would alight.

And then he thrust by a crag and came out by a hole,

whirling out of the rocks with a fell weapon,

a Danish axe new honed, for dealing the blow,

with a biting blade bow-bent to the haft,

ground on a grindstone, four feet broad –

no less, by that love-lace gleaming full bright.

And the giant in green was garbed as at first,

both the looks and the legs, the locks and the beard,

save that firm on his feet he finds his ground,

sets the haft to the stones and stalks beside it.

When he came to the water, he would not wade,

he hopped over on his axe and boldly he strides,

blazing with wrath, on a bit of field broad about

in snow.

Sir Gawain the man did greet,

he bowed to him, nothing low;

the other said: 'Now, Sir Sweet,

men may trust your word, I owe.'

90

'Gawain,' quoth the green man, 'God may you guard!
Indeed you are welcome, knight, to my place,
and you have timed your travel as true man should.
And you know the covenant pledged between us:
at this time twelvemonth gone you took what befell,
that I should at this New Year promptly requite.
And we are in this valley verily alone;
here are no ranks to sever us, serve as you will.
Heft your helm off your head, and have here your pay.
Ask no more debate than I did of you then
when you whipped off my head at a single blow.'
'Nay, by God,' quoth Gawain, 'who lent me a soul,
I shall bear you no grudge for the grief that befalls.
Strike but the one stroke, and I shall stand still
and offer no hindrance, come work as you like,
                    I swear.'
            He leant down his neck, and bowed,
            and showed the white flesh all bare,
            as if he were no way cowed;
            for to shrink he would not dare.

'Heft your helm off your head, and have here your pay'
The Boy's King Arthur (p38, 1922)
Sidney Lanier (1842-1881), Newell Convers Wyeth (1882-1945)
Wikimedia Commons

91

hen the man in green readies him swiftly,

girds up his grim blade, to smite Gawain;

with all the strength in his body he bears it aloft,

manages it mightily as if he would mar him.

Had he driven it down as direly as he aimed,

one had been dead of the deed who was dauntless ever.

But Gawain glanced at the grim blade sideways,

as it came gliding down on him to destroy him,

and his shoulders shrank a little from the sharp edge.

The other man with a shrug the slice withholds,

and then reproves the prince with many proud words:

'You are not Gawain,' quoth the man, 'held so great,

that was never afraid of the host by hill or by vale,

for now you flinch for fear ere you feel harm.

Such cowardice of that knight have I never heard.

I neither flinched nor fled, friend, when you let fly,

nor cast forth any quibble in King Arthur's house.

My head flew off, at my feet, yet fled I never;

yet you, ere any harm haps, are fearful at heart.

And I ought to be branded the better man, I say,

therefore.'

Quoth Gawain: 'I flinched once,

Yet so will I no more;

Though if my head fall on the stones,

I cannot it restore.'

92

'e brisk, man, by your faith, and bring me to the point.

Deal me my destiny and do it out of hand,

for I shall stand your stroke, and start no more

till your axe has hit me – have here my troth.'

'Have at you, then,' quoth the other, and heaves it aloft

and glares as angrily as if he were mad.

He menaces him mightily, but touches him not,

swiftly withholding his hand ere it might hurt.

Gawain gravely it bides and moves not a muscle,

but stands still as a stone or the stump of a tree

that is riven in rocky ground with roots a hundred.

Then merrily again he spoke, the man in green:

'So now you have your heart whole, it me behoves.

Hold you safe now the knighthood Arthur gave you,

and keep your neck from this cut, if ever it may!'

Gawain full fiercely with anger then said:

'Why, thrash on, you wild man, threaten no longer;

it seems your heart is warring with your own self.'

'Forsooth,' quoth the other, 'so fiercely you speak,

I'll not a moment longer delay your errand

> I vow.'

>> Then he takes up his stance to strike

>> pouts lips and puckers his brow;

>> Nothing there for him to like

>> who hopes for no rescue now.

93

p the weapon lifts lightly, is let down fair,
and the blade's border beside the bare neck.
Though heaved heavily it hurt him not more,
but nicked him on the one side, and severed the skin.
The sharp edge sank in the flesh through the fair fat,
so that bright blood over his shoulders shot to the earth.
And when the knight saw his blood blotting the snow,
he spurted up, feet first, more than a spear-length,
seized swiftly his helm and on his head cast it,
shrugged with his shoulders his fine shield under,
broke out his bright sword, and bravely he spoke –
never since he was a babe born of his mother
had he ever in this world a heart half so blithe –
'Back man, with your blade, and brandish no more!
I have received a stroke in this place without strife,
and if you offer another I'll readily requite you
and yield it you swiftly again – of that be you sure –
        as foe.
    But one stroke to me here falls;
    the covenant stated so,
    arranged in Arthur's halls,
    so lay your weapon, now, low!'

94

he other then turned away and on his axe rested,

set the haft to the earth and leant on the head,

and looked at the lord who held to his ground,

how doughty, and dread-less, enduring he stands

armed, without awe; in his heart he him liked.

Then he spoke merrily in a mighty voice,

and with a ringing roar to the knight he said:

'Bold man be not so fierce in this field.

No man here has mistreated you, been unmannerly,

nor behaved but by covenant at King's court made.

I hit with a stroke, and you have it, and are well paid;

I release you from the rest of all other rights.

If I had been livelier, a buffet perchance

I could have worked more wilfully, to bring you anger.

First I menaced you merrily with a single feint,

and rent you with no riving cut, rightly offered

for the pledge that we made on the very first night;

for you truthfully kept troth and dealt with me true,

all the gain you gave me, as good men should.

The next blow for the morn, man, I proffered;

you kissed my fair wife, the kisses were mine.

For both these days I brought you but two bare feints,

without scathe.

Truth for the truth restore,

then man need dread no wraith.

On the third you failed for sure,

and so took that blow, in faith.'

95

'or it is mine that you wear, that same woven girdle;

my own wife gave it you, I know it well forsooth.

Now, know I well your kisses and conduct too,

and the wooing of my wife; I wrought it myself.

I sent her to test you, and truly I think you

the most faultless man that was ever afoot.

As a pearl beside whitened pea is more precious,

so is Gawain, in good faith, beside other good knights.

But here sir you lacked a little, wanting in loyalty;

but that was for no wily work, nor wooing neither,

but for love of your life – so I blame you the less.'

The other strong man in study stood a great while,

so aggrieved that for grief he grimaced within.

All the blood of his breast burnt in his face,

that he shrank for shame at all the man said.

The first words the knight could frame on that field:

'Curse upon cowardice and covetousness both!

In you are villainy and vice that virtue distress.'

Then he caught at the knot and pulled it loose,

and fair flung the belt at the man himself:

'Lo! There's the falseness, foul may it fall!

For fear of your knock cowardice me taught

to accord with covetousness, forsake my kind,

the largesse and loyalty that belongs to knights.

Now am I faulted and false, and ever a-feared;

from both treachery and untruth come sorrow

and care!

I confess to you knight, here, still,

my fault in this affair;

let me understand your will,

and henceforth I shall beware.'

96

hen laughed that other lord and lightly said:

'I hold it happily made whole, the harm that I had;

You are confessed so clean, cleared of your faults,

and have done penance plain at the point of my blade,

I hold you absolved of that sin, as pure and as clean,

as though you were never at fault since first you were born.

And I give you, sir, the girdle that is gold-hemmed.

As it is green as my gown, Sir Gawain, you may

think upon this same trial when you throng forth

among princes of price, and this the pure token

of the test at the Green Chapel to chivalrous knights.

And you shall this New Year come back to my castle,

and we shall revel away the remnant of this rich feast

      I mean'

     Thus urged him hard the lord,

     and said: 'With my wife, I ween,

     we shall bring you in accord,

     who was your enemy keen.'

97

ay, forsooth,' quoth the knight, and seized his helm

doffed it deliberately, and dealt his thanks:

'I have sojourned enough. May luck you betide,

and may He yield you reward that rewards all men!

And commend me to the courteous, your comely wife,

both the one and the other, my honoured ladies,

that thus their knight with a trick have cunningly beguiled.

But it is no wonder for a fool to run mad

and through wiles of woman be won to sorrow.

For so was Adam on earth with one beguiled,

and Solomon with many such, Samson too –

Delilah dealt him his doom – and David thereafter

was blinded by Bathsheba, and suffered much ill.

Since these were wounded with wiles, it were wise

to love them well and believe them not, if a lord could.

For these were the finest formerly, favoured by fate

excellently of all those under heaven's rule

       ill used;

    And all these were beguiled

    with women that they used.

    If I am now beguiled

    I think I should be excused.'

98

'For your girdle,' quoth Gawain, 'God reward you!
That I will wear with good will, not for the white gold,
nor the stuff, the silk, nor the slender pendants,
its worth, nor richness, nor for the fine working;
but as a sign of my sin I shall see it often
when I ride in renown, remorseful, remembering
the fault and the frailty of perverse flesh,
how it tends to entice to the tarnish of sin.
And thus when pride shall stir me in prowess of arms,
one look at this love-lace shall lower my heart.
But one thing I would you pray, displease you never:
Since you are lord of yonder land where I lingered
Say you by your knighthood – may He reward you
that upholds the heavens and on high sits –
how you tell your true name, and then no more?'
'That shall I tell you truly,' quoth the other then,
'Bertilak de Hautdesert I am in this land,
through might of Morgan la Faye, that dwells in my house,
and is mistress of magic, by crafts well learned
the mysteries of Merlin, many has she taken,
for she has dealt in depths full dearly sometime
with that excellent sage, and that know all your knights
        at home.
    Morgan the Goddess
    therefore is now her name;
    none has such high haughtiness
    that she cannot make full tame.'

'*None has such high haughtiness that she cannot make full
tame*'
The Romance of King Arthur and his Knights of the Round
Table (p76, 1917)
Sir Thomas Malory (15th cent), Alfred William Pollard (1859-
1944), Arthur Rackham (1867-1939)
Internet Archive Book Images

99

'he sent me in this same wise to your wide hall

for to assay its pride, test if all that were truth

that runs on the great renown of the Round Table.

She worked all this wonder your wits to ravel,

to grieve Guinevere and to bring her to die

aghast at that same ghoul with his ghostly speech

with his head in his hand before the high table.

That is she that is at home, the ancient lady;

she is even your aunt, Arthur's half-sister,

daughter of Tintagel's Duchess that dear Uther after

had Arthur upon, who now is your king.

Therefore, sir, I entreat you, come to your aunt,

make merry in my house. My men do love you,

and I wish you as well, man, by my faith,

as any man under God, for your great truth.'

Yet Gawain denied him, nay, he would in no way.

They clasped and kissed, commending each other

to the Prince of Paradise, parted in the cold where

they stood.

Gawain on steed I ween

to the King goes fast as he could,

and the man in the emerald green

whithersoever he would.

100

ild ways in the world Gawain now rides,

on Gringolet, he whom grace had gifted with life.

Often he harboured in houses, and often outside,

had adventures much in the vales, often vanquisher,

that I do not at this time intend to recall.

The hurt was all whole that he had in his neck,

and the bright belt he bore all thereabout,

obliquely, as a baldric, bound at his side,

tied under his left arm, the lace, with a knot,

as token he was tainted with guilt of his fault.

And so he comes to the court, all safe and sound.

Delight dawned in that dwelling when the great knew

that good Gawain was come; and thought it gain.

The King kisses the knight, and the queen also,

and then many staunch knights sought to salute him,

to know how he had fared; and faithfully he tells

confessing all the cost of the cares he had suffered –

what chanced at the chapel, the cast of its lord,

the love of the lady, the lace at the last.

The nick in the neck he naked them showed,

that he had for his lie, from the lord's hands,

in blame.

He was pained he must tell,

he groaned for grief at the same;

blood ran to his face pell-mell,

when he showed the mark, for shame.

'And so he comes to the court, all safe and sound'
The Book of Romance (p160, 1902)
Andrew Land (1844-1912)
Internet Archive Book Images

101

'o, Lord!' quoth the knight, and handled the lace,
'This is the belt of blame I bear at my neck,
this is the hurt and the harm that I have learned
through the cowardice and covetousness I caught there.
This is the token of the untruth I am taken in,
and I must needs it wear while I may last.
For none may hide harm done, and go unscathed,
for where it is once attached depart will it never.'
The King comforts the knight, and all the court also,
laughing loudly thereat, and lovingly agreeing,
those lords and ladies that belonged to the Table,
that each born to the brotherhood, a baldric should have,
a belt, oblique him about, of a bright green,
and that for the sake of the knight, the same hue.
For it was accorded to the renown of the Round Table,
and he that had it was honoured, evermore after,
as is borne out by the best book of romance.
Thus in Arthur's day this adventure was tried,
the books of Brutus thereof bear witness.
Since Brutus, the bold baron, first bent hither,
after the siege and assault had ceased at Troy,

> there is,

> many an adventure born
> befallen such, ere this.
> Now who bears the crown of thorn,
> May He bring us to his bliss! **AMEN.**

HONY SOYT QUI MAL PENCE

About The Translator

nthony Kline lives in England. He graduated in Mathematics from the University of Manchester, and was Chief Information Officer (Systems Director) of a large UK Company, before dedicating himself to his literary work and interests. He was born in 1947. His work consists of translations of poetry; critical works, biographical history with poetry as a central theme; and his own original poetry. He has translated into English from Latin, Ancient Greek, Classical Chinese and the European languages. He also maintains a deep interest in developments in Mathematics and the Sciences.

He continues to write predominantly for the Internet, making all works available in download format, with an added focus on the rapidly developing area of electronic books. His most extensive works are complete translations of Ovid's Metamorphoses and Dante's Divine Comedy.

Made in the USA
Columbia, SC
23 August 2024

41054670R00089